Manipulation

Learn the Art of Influencing People Through the Most Powerful Techniques of Persuasion, Mind Control, NLP, and Other Psychological Techniques for Reading and Persuading Anyone

Table of Contents

Introduction

No sensible driver would let one of his passengers take the steering wheel to drive in his place and go wherever he wants. This is what happens every time we are harassed or manipulated. Brutally or insidiously, someone requires us to think, act, live, or love as he or she wants. By using techniques that paralyze us, confuse us, or prevent us from reacting, the manipulator invades and thus destroys an important part of our life. When you are happy and confident one day, then irritable, anxious, or apathetic on another day, you may think that life is so unfair. You may begin to whine, feel sorry for yourself or collapse, and feel distressed and alone. But that does not change anything that preoccupies or overwhelms you.

It is normal to experience moments of discouragement, for example when one is overworked or, on the contrary, when one is afraid of being deprived of work. It is equally legitimate to lack confidence or to have doubts when faced with failure, conflict, illness, or an apparently hopeless situation. But often these symptoms are also a direct result of some form of manipulation.

Some manipulations are so hidden or perverse that often the victim cannot detect the origin. She accuses herself wrongly and looks into how she might be responsible for what happened to her. Conversely, other manipulations are quite predictable, but we also know that we will not be able to resist the manipulator and that we will eventually give in to him.

This book is intended for all those who are tired of walking on their feet, enough to be too kind or too good, enough not to be able to live their lives, enough to be unhappy. In a nutshell, this book is for anyone who is tired of being manipulated.

Manipulating or being manipulated is not inevitable. No one is obliged to spend his life following or suffering the will of one or the other. It is possible to change and to let go without reacting. To better defend yourself and to avoid blaming yourself for being too kind, too good or too confident, this book has two objectives:

- The first is to discover, through numerous examples, the different aspects of manipulation which have been classified in a clear and precise way. It is indeed essential to know the symptoms and the mechanisms of the various types of manipulation if one hopes to be able to defend oneself effectively.

- The second objective of this book is to provide ammunition to all those who feel harassed or who feel manipulated (in one way or another) without knowing how to defend themselves or get out of the trap in which they fell. We will discover in the various chapters all the techniques used by the manipulators as well as the means to resist them.

The information and the many exercises and tools contained in these pages are for those who really want to put them into practice. Let everyone retain what best suits them to get rid of what is bothering them and thus live a free and happy life.

Chapter 1 - Three Types of Manipulation

Before you can solve any problem, you must first identify it and find out what it is. The words manipulation and harassment are becoming more and more common. The media always talks about electoral manipulation, manipulation of capital, or manipulation of public opinion. The spotlight of the news, once focused on sexual harassment, is now focused on moral harassment.

Manipulation has many faces, sometimes very familiar. The buddy who invites himself unexpectedly (without worrying about the possible inconvenience) or someone who regularly borrows tools, books, or money without ever returning them to us are manipulators. The colleague who gets the project or the position that would typically have been given to us, the girlfriend who always ridicules what we do or finally, an individual with whom a conversation puts "our morale in the socks." Are these people inevitable? Are there people more sensitive than others to manipulation? Is it an evil that we have to endure by clenching our teeth, or can we do something to avoid manipulators and defend ourselves?

Before we can answer these questions, we must begin by knowing what manipulation is, what it is made of, and how it works. Starting from these solid bases, we will be able to discover the means and the tools to be implemented so as not to be manipulated anymore.

Basically, there are three types of manipulation that are distinguished from each other by the specific intent of the manipulator.

- In the first type of manipulation, the intention of the manipulator is always good, useful, or pleasant for the one who is the victim.

- In a second manipulative mode, the intent of the manipulator is egocentric. The manipulator turns the world around his personal interests, without worrying about the consequences for his victims.

- The intent of the manipulator, in the third kind of manipulation, is paranoid and always aims at a destructive and malicious purpose.

Positive Manipulation (Type I)

The intention of positive manipulation is consistently good, useful, or enjoyable. Even if it is not really manipulation in the sense that we usually hear it, it is essential to talk about it, if only to better perceive the other dubious types of manipulation that are hidden behind naive appearances.

Giving a gift or a pleasant surprise to someone is a type I manipulation, but offering an empty box to a child for his birthday and laughing loudly at his disappointment is not a type I manipulation even if the adult claims the opposite. This first type of manipulation (as its name suggests) always contains a positive intention; it's the opposite of blackmail. Even when a parent is pushing hard to get his child to wash his teeth regularly or when a nurse is giving a comforting speech with a syringe in her hand (do not be afraid, you will not feel anything), the intention remains good and aims in the direction of good, better, pleasant or useful. Sweet persuasion is a kind of positive manipulation.

A mother can persuade her child who is reluctant to work by saying: "If you finish your morning assignment, you will have all the afternoon to do what you like, otherwise you will spend the day unhappy." We can also manipulate someone by showing the positive aspects of something that displeases them. "Listen, I cannot go home on time because I have to stay in the office... I know it's boring, but it will allow me to go home earlier on Friday and have a better weekend."

Whether it's called bargaining, diplomacy, negotiation, mere advice, or persuasion, it's always about manipulation. But this corresponds to a type I manipulation because the intention starts from the heart and the manipulator seeks the good of the person who is the object of the manipulation.

If, on the other hand, you are made to believe that something is good for you when you know or feel the opposite, be certain that it is not a type I manipulation. Read on to stop letting yourself go!

Egocentric Manipulation (Type II)

The intention that guides the egocentric manipulator is the search for his own personal benefit. He thinks only of his interests, without worrying about the inconvenience, embarrassment, or discomfort that his behavior may cause others. The type II manipulator is trivial, cunning, deceitful, resourceful, and talkative. He is often guided by the lure of material gain, power, or fame; thinking only of himself, he always acts selfishly.

Type II manipulation is the kind we are subjected to when we are deceived, manipulated or trapped by someone who seeks to acquire something that he could not otherwise obtain.

Jean-Pierre, who had no particular qualifications, but who possessed a lot of charm and who knew how to speak, went door-to-door to sell encyclopedias. He was very successful because he had discovered that he was very convincing to the elderly who, trusting his good looks, signed the contract without knowing what they were engaging in. He was not worried about whether their low incomes would allow them to pay bills that amounted to more than a month's salary. The essential thing for him was to have contracts; that was his livelihood.

The type II manipulator is that friend who asks us for a service or money by making sure that we cannot refuse him. He is also the one who, to show his spirit, cracks jokes and laughs without knowing how to stop when it becomes offensive. He is also the employee who puts a spoke in the wheel of his colleagues to get a promotion in their place. He is the teacher who terrifies his class to prove his power, or he is the journalist who dramatizes a subject to be certain that his report will get airtime ahead of his competitors. None of these characters act maliciously. Basically, they do not want to hurt anyone. No, they simply focus on their personal interests without thinking or worrying too much about the consequences.

A lot of quarrels or separations are due to this type of manipulator. It is the "macho" husband who wants to show his authority and his independence by doing only what interests him, without taking into account the expectations of his wife. In trying to prove that he is the leader and that no one can command him, he does not see the upheavals that his behavior causes towards his companion. This man who thinks that he is so perfect will be surprised one day to see her go. Conversely, the woman who regularly contradicts or devalues her husband in public to show that she is not a submissive woman and that she has character turns out to be a manipulator.

Politicians who make promises and who, once elected, do not hold them, are type II manipulators, just like companies who relocate by dismissing their staff simply to increase profits. The latter think only of their interests, without worrying about future social disasters.

Marketing is fond of egocentric manipulations, as shown by the following example (an experiment conducted by researchers in social psychology).

When being offered a sample of pizza at the entrance to the supermarket, one in two agreed to taste it. But if the demonstrator touched their arm while making his proposal, two out of three accepted his offer.

Nobody has a rational explanation to explain this phenomenon, but to touch the arm of someone when making an offer is a small cause producing great effects, especially for the manipulator.

This last example shows us that some manipulations do not necessarily have harmful consequences. Unfortunately, most of our inconvenience comes from egocentric manipulations that we did not know how to prevent or that we could not resist.

Sylvie receives her old aunt who has asked to spend a few days at her home. But in accepting (or rather refraining from refusing this request), she could not imagine the nature of the visit. Starting the first evening, the aunt said to Sylvie:

"Tomorrow we will start by visiting this exhibition which opens at 10 am, and then we will go eat in your usual restaurant. This way I'll see where you work and then you'll be able to use your coupons at restaurants. In the afternoon, we will go to the department stores and in the evening we will end up in a tea room because I love tea. You know, I have not been in town for a long time, and it's a great pleasure for me to spend a few days with you."

Sylvie tries to protest, to explain that she cannot be free so easily, but her aunt does not let her speak and explains to her that she feels so lonely since her husband's death. Sylvie, touched, does not know what to say and her aunt takes the opportunity to add: "Come on! By the way, what are we eating for dinner? You know, I usually do not eat much at night, but for the time I'm with you, we could enjoy it. I'll let you choose the restaurant, I'm not difficult and as long as it's not too noisy, everything suits me."

Whether they are small rogues, marketers, politicians, companies, little bosses, selfish colleagues or "macho" husbands, the type II manipulator acts primarily to satisfy his interests. He does not intend to harm anyone. Totally focused on what he wants, he does not see or refuses to see the real damage that his behavior generates. However, we can discuss their actions with them and change their minds by focusing on their intellectual honesty.

Malicious Manipulation (Type III)

With this third type, we enter the field of the sneaky. This conscious and deliberate attempt to destroy others is extremely dangerous. Indeed, if the intention of the first type of manipulator is positive and that of the second selfish, the intention of the third manipulator is destruction.

The latter does not want the good of anybody, and he does not necessarily seek his personal interest. His sole and main purpose is to destroy what threatens him or what seems to be intolerable or hateful. We can sum up the intention of this manipulator by saying that everything he undertakes is intended to kill you, to ruin what you do, or to destroy an aspect of your personality that does not suit him.

The Two Characteristics of Type III Manipulation

This manipulation is characterized by malevolent and perverse intent as well as concealment of his attacks.

A Malicious and Perverse Intention

When he harms someone, the malicious manipulator often claims the opposite and claims that he is acting for the good of his victim or for a just cause. Malicious intent often hides behind apparent honesty.

Michael is an educator and cares for handicapped children. One day, he receives the unpleasant surprise of seeing the police enter his class to ask him questions because his wife, a manipulator with whom he is undergoing a divorce, accused him of having incestuous relations with his little girls between 6 and 8 years old. He defends himself and tries to explain that he has done nothing. But, to get custody of the children, his wife picks up and uses everything he says to "push" him further.

She pretends to act in the interest of her children. The accusation was, of course, unfounded, but the case still lasted several years during which it was totally impossible for Michael to meet his daughters without the presence of a social worker. He spent all his savings, lost all his property, his house, his car, his furniture, and went into debt to pay a lawyer. Because of his wife's false accusation, he was forbidden to work with minors and he lost his job. After several years of counseling, totally ruined and completely "demolished" both morally and physically, he is finally identified as innocent. The damage is done, and his life is broken. The manipulator has won on all fronts.

Hiding the Attacks

The manipulator always manages to destroy his victims without being noticed by them. He destroys but conceals it from those he seeks to defeat. This type of manipulation is like a silent and faceless destruction for those who do not know or do not want to see it.

Laurie is a chef and has lunch every day at noon with Myrtille, a colleague and friend. They take advantage of these moments of relaxation to talk about things and also to exchange ideas or advice when they encounter particular difficulties. Gradually, Laurie is sidelined and her responsibilities melt like snow in the sun. After having regularly reproached her for baseless misconduct, her supervisor removes all of her supervisory responsibilities and assigns her to a position where she has no one to manage.

For a long time, she tried to understand what had happened to her. She often talked with Myrtille about what her boss was doing to her. She tried, but to no avail, to find an explanation and to uncover the reasons for her downfall. She felt guilty and lost confidence in herself. One day, finally, she noticed that her "friend" Myrtille was now handling her former duties and taking over from the projects she had initiated. Laurie realized, a little late, the origin of her misfortune.

The Manipulator

The manipulator is a person with excessive pride who does not respect the other person and tries to prevent them from living in their own way. His goal is to diminish, belittle, or even destroy his victims. To achieve his goal, he uses misinformation, lies, or slander.

For an attentive observer, it is evident that he sows the seeds of trouble around him and that he puts people against each other. He is an expert in moral harassment who rarely intervenes directly, preferring to push others to act in his place. He is a coward who makes his victims feel responsible for and guilty of what he does to them, and that allows him to continue to destroy all innocence.

One can hardly impress him, nor have a hold on him. He seems unassailable and unshakable; he knows everything. We would like to be able to defend ourselves and counter-attack, but as he terrorizes people, they do not succeed or do not dare. When they try something, it usually turns against them, thus seeming to prove their persecutor right.

He says he is honest and fair, acting for your good or for a good cause. This defense system implies that he will never recognize his wrongs. When he is caught, he regrets nothing; he does not apologize and feels no compassion for his victims. He is very often obsessed with the idea of being in danger. This threat is so real to him that it allows him to justify and legitimize his evil deeds. This is how people are led to kill and torture in the name of their faith, their convictions, or their anxieties. They can even be proud of it.

A Monster!

It is hard to imagine that human beings can be so mean and hateful. A normal, healthy person has great difficulty in conceiving that such destructive and harmful intentions can be fostered. It's just as foolish as imagining oneself killing, torturing, or raping. However, in the same way that there are murderers, executioners, or rapists, there are also malevolent beings that spread evil around them.

To think that such individuals do not exist in our environment or to believe that they will get bored and stop their destruction process to change their strategy is an illusion. Worse, this error of judgment strengthens the manipulator and makes him even more formidable for anyone who believes such nonsense.

It is the ambiguity that exists between his speech and his action that makes the Type III manipulator extremely dangerous. The latter may very well have a pleasant appearance and make reassuring remarks while acting in the shadows to put people against each other and generate significant conflicts. A manipulator can be appreciated by his entourage and, at the same time, adopt behaviors that are quite hateful and ignored by all.

Eleonore, 32, a senior executive in a big company, is regularly beaten by a jealous husband who wants to make her confess that she is cheating on him. She often wears sunglasses and appropriate clothing so that one notices the marks of the blows she has received. Like many battered women, she does not trust anyone, lest her husband attacks her children. And she loves her companion and does not want to leave him. Eleonore wishes to continue her life as a couple and family. Over time, the situation seems hopeless, and she eventually sinks into depression.

One of the most common results of this type of manipulation is the feeling of guilt that overwhelms the victim. By concealing what is going on and what she is going through, she becomes, in a way the accomplice of her executioner.

This manipulation is, in many ways, monstrous. It is difficult to denounce because of the feeling of guilt already mentioned. This is often the fate of children who have suffered incest or acts of pedophilia. To the victim, the feeling of guilt is generally imposed by the manipulator: "It's your fault, it's you who pushed me to do that." Guilt slowly makes its way into the victim's mind and leads her to believe that she deserves her suffering, and the manipulator is right to behave as he does or that he is acting in her best interest.

Who Is He?

He has an anonymous, everyday face. He can be the father of a family who keeps his wife and children under an iron fist. He crushes them under his tyrannical law; he prevents them from thinking and living for themselves or taking any initiative. At the same time, he says loudly that he is a responsible parent who thinks and acts only for the good of his family. This is the case of a man who managed to prevent, discreetly and repeatedly, the marriage of his daughter to boys who, according to him, were not good enough for her.

How Does He Act?

The manipulator is obstinate like the waves of the ocean. He never stops on the road to his goals and will stop at nothing to destroy what he believes to be a threat or a danger because he has the conviction to fight for the right cause. The manipulator uses a real arsenal. Insidious and devaluing remarks, indelicate comments and lies, along with jokes and regular mockery make up a subset of his weapons that weaken and undermine the morale of the person he or she is aiming for.

Carole is a little overweight. One of her colleagues noticed it and, at each meeting, did not fail to make an innocuous remark to her: "You look good today... Your dress fits you very well, and it hides your hips well... Are you planning to go on a diet this summer or are you leaving in September? Have you thought of having yourself operated on? So take a little cake..." It makes others laugh, but not Carole who simply pretends to have fun with others. In the evening, when she finds herself alone in her apartment, she is desperate because of her weakness and her inability to go on a diet. So she cries and consoles herself by binge eating.

The manipulator is cruel; he likes to hurt by criticizing, mocking or belittling his victim, but of course, he does not at all support being subjected to what he imposes on others. He likes to control, but cannot stand that we can control him in one way or another. From his point of view, he thinks that what happens to you is of little importance, but what happens to him is, on the other hand, always very serious.

The manipulator acts with skill. He leads a secret, faceless war and conceals his maneuvers so well that sometimes his victims are completely wrong. In this case, as long as he is not really unmasked, he will continue his work of destruction, pulling strings without anyone noticing.

Aurélie and Baptiste have been married for more than twelve years. But in recent years, they have frequent disputes. Aurélie reproaches him, in particular, for thinking only of his work, for not taking enough care of the children, and for leaving her in charge of the house. When things get too heated, they calm down, take time to explain themselves and find common ground. But, invariably, the same problems reappear in a slightly different form. Today, the situation has become so serious that they have come to consider divorce proceedings.

In desperation, they decide to get help from a professional. Very quickly, it appears that disputes arise most often after a visit or a phone call from the mother-in-law. As they continue their reflection, they discover how the mother-in-law insidiously adds oil to the fire by inducing her daughter to harass her husband because she is jealous to see them happy, while she herself is on the verge of her third divorce.

After understanding who was manipulating them, it was easy for them to respect a few simple rules to lead a calm and harmonious life.

The manipulator acts insidiously, and this is the extent of his objective. Type III manipulation is an obscure and cruel world in which the manipulator really intends to harm, injure or destroy a person, a family, a service, a company, or even a country or a civilization (such is the case for international terrorists). In the shadows, he continues his work of undermining, hiding behind the deceptive appearances of purity, innocence, fragility, or friendly presence.

The manipulator is a virus. He is similar to cancer cells that develop silently by slowly and systematically destroying the defense system of his victims until they crumble and are unable to react. Most often, when one discovers his presence, it is already too late.

"After my dismissal, I put all my savings into this small printing press. Since I did not know the technique, I trusted the employees completely. At first, everything worked well. I had customers and orders arrived regularly. I hired new employees and then suddenly, I realized that nothing was working anymore. I do not know how it happened, but there was a lot of sick leave and one employee was even dead. Due to incomprehensible errors, some work had to be redone at our expense. A machine burned, but we do not really understand why. Finally, we lost more and more customers because of rumors circulating about the company.

My morale is low. One day, I feel determined to fight the bad luck and then, the next day, I do not see any way out. I feel like I'll never make it and I feel guilty for missing something. I want to give up everything... I feel hopeless. Recently, I took my car and drove down the highway for four hundred kilometers without knowing where I was going. When I realized that I was trying to suppress myself, I stopped and cried for two hours. After hiring an outside consultant, it quickly became apparent that two people were systematically involved in each incident. Then, the lie detector test made it possible to identify, with certainty, the true manipulator. Finally, using and implementing some simple rules and principles, the problem was quickly solved and business resumed."

It is not a question of wondering if this is possible, or even if such characters exist. The question is how to identify them in order to avoid them. The tests in the third chapter are there to help the reader know for sure who is causing the trouble and how to attack him. It will be much easier to defend oneself and to use the tools presented in this book.

Beware of Confusion!

The mere reading of a medical encyclopedia leads to the certainty of you having the disease. You may feel the symptoms and most people will go to see a doctor. This phenomenon is common among medical students and students of psychiatry or psychology.

Type III manipulation is a heavy and troubling subject that tends to confuse the person who approaches it. This is why some readers might begin to think that they are surrounded by manipulation. They might also suspect everyone of wanting to harass them as soon as they get upset or are simply contradicted. This way of posing as a victim only aggravates things and attracts trouble as the lightning rod attracts lightning.

Type III manipulation, including moral harassment, is based on the manipulator's original desire to harm or destroy.

Benedict has the impression that his director no longer trusts him and that she is seeking his departure. This restricts his activities and controls everything he does; he neglects to inform her of what she should know and does not take into account what she says. At the slightest difficulty, be it a lost file or when something is wrong, he begins to feel guilty.

Benedict, once so efficient, is now completely discouraged. He feels depressed, despised, humiliated, and cannot hold back tears when he talks about his situation. He tries to defend himself, but the more he attacks the problem, the more he feels overwhelmed by what is happening to him, and the less he feels that he can escape this state of moral harassment that he has found himself in. One day, he accidentally learns that his boss is trying to get him to leave, not because she wants to destroy him, but simply because she wants to hire her boyfriend in his place.

From this day, Benedict is transformed. He realizes that it's his director who has a problem and he has nothing to reproach himself for! Thus, the discovery of the true intention of the leader transforms a formidable type III manipulation into a simple type II manipulation.

Instead of keeping himself in the position of a victim and thus getting into trouble, he stops doubting himself. As he stops thinking "moral harassment" he emotionally escapes his boss's attacks. He is no longer paralyzed by this terrible sensation of being the prey of a perverse destroyer who only thinks of eliminating him.

Moral harassment is a kind of type III manipulation that must be recognized and unmasked. However, it is easy to err and accuse someone wrongly, forgetting to take into account the true intent of the manipulator. This requires knowing how to broaden one's field of vision.

"I left him because I felt he was preventing me from living. When he was there, it was as if I did not have enough air to breathe. I left him only after I learned he had a mistress. If I had known earlier, I would have certainly felt less guilty and I could have spoken with him to try to understand what was wrong between us. It might not have changed the result, but at least I wouldn't have felt so bad during that time. We would certainly have separated more serenely."

Chapter 2 - Recognize a Manipulator

One might think that manipulators are easy to recognize and that their actions are enough to unmask them. Unfortunately, things are not so simple. Even if the manipulation is easy to spot in others, it is much less obvious when one is himself a victim. It is enough to commit to memory that it often takes a certain time to realize that we have been manipulated.

Whatever the intention that guides him, the manipulator is clever at hiding his maneuvers. Whether Type II or Type III, it mixes true and false, sincerity and duplicity, spontaneity and calculation. His attitudes and behavior are often difficult to perceive for an untrained eye; he knows how to surround himself with enough mystery to deceive the world.

By describing the behaviors and attitudes most common to different types of manipulation, this chapter wants to make the reader become much more attentive to the slightest signal of danger. Without falling into paranoia and seeing manipulators everywhere, the goal is to acquire enough information to no longer be fooled by remaining deaf and blind in the face of obvious symptoms.

Detection of either of these symptoms should be enough to alert our attention and arouse our suspicion. But we must be careful not to fall into the opposite extreme by accusing others without cause. Someone who is healthy can sometimes adopt manipulative behavior; that does not make them a dangerous person.

A true manipulator is distinguished by his intention as well as by the constant and regular use he makes of one or many of the behaviors we are going to describe.

Recognize him in his particular way of communicating:

- He speaks in a roundabout way.

- He never says anything categorically, but he is very adept at talking about what's wrong and sowing doubt in the minds of those who listen.

A good manipulator spreads rumors or conveys the worst calumnies in a natural way and without ever "seeming to touch it". In these conditions, it is difficult to imagine that he could be the author.

He Loves Gossiping

While he usually neglects to pass on the good news, the manipulator retains all the bad things that come within his reach. He amplifies them before transmitting them to others, with delight.

Julie talks to her friends about a former colleague they knew and she came across by chance: "Now it seems that he earns much more than us, but he is still on the move and cannot see his family anymore. If you want my opinion, his marriage will not last very long, you cannot be both the oven and mitt... Well, that's what everyone says! "

He Clearly Expresses What He Is Usually Told

He passes messages under the guise of pretense, feigning naivety or inattention. "Oh, excuse me, I am still confused. I'm so sorry..." For example, this may be said by a manipulator to hide the harm she has done by releasing, apparently inadvertently, information she should have kept quiet.

He Only Mentions Generalities

The manipulator is a disinformation specialist who is practiced at spreading his gossip but hiding that he created it by saying: "It is said that... It seems that... Everyone knows that... ". In this way, one can believe that he is only repeating what everyone knows or ought to know. This way of never saying I, gives more weight and (false) truth to his remarks.

To generalize information makes it more solid, more credible, and above all an orphan because the one who receives it does not think of putting it in doubt and forgets from where he received this news. This is how rumors are born whose origin we no longer know.

Jean is a representative in armored doors. He is also a type II manipulator who succeeds very professionally because he knows enough to worry the people he visits by asserting unverifiable generalities: "Everyone knows that we are no longer safe, nowadays... No one can believe that they are safe from burglaries... You must have noticed, too, that there is more and more aggression around you... "After creating a climate of fear, it is very easy for Jean to offer his products and win a new customer who will soon thank him for being so well protected.

He is only interested in him. He can tell you about his problems for hours without you being able to put a word in or get rid of him. He is also able to preach falsehood to know the truth and puts his victims to sleep under an uninterrupted stream of words.

Léa works in a big administration and she has a way of getting information without asking direct questions. Thus, every time she sees a new head, she says with great assurance: "So you're the new accountant!" The other then justifies himself immediately and restores the truth by saying, "Oh no, I just got hired to the IT department." Then Leah begins her manipulating business, distorting the information she transmits as follows: "It seems they have hired a new person in the IT department. They are always the ones who benefit from additional staff. We are always the same, we just have to manage and we always do more with fewer people. "

He Does Not Appreciate What Is Clear and Simple

In his desire to show that he knows everything about everything, the manipulator opposes without understanding anything. He does not make any decisions. On the other hand, he knows how to criticize what others are doing and point out dysfunctions.

Thierry is well settled, whether in his work or with his family. He never proposes anything original and waits for others to make a commitment to look for what is wrong, to send comments, or to launch criticism. On the road, when "she" is driving, he keeps on commenting: "Be careful! Accelerate, you'll never be able to cross here... Watch your rearview mirror... Don't turn so close!" If she chooses to take a road and they experience a traffic jam, he will blame her choice by saying, "I don't mean to cause any trouble, but I would never have taken this route because everyone knows that we must not go through here."

Remember

A manipulator is very good at talking about what's wrong and sowing doubt in the minds of others. He speaks only by generalities; he does not know how to listen and does not take responsibility for his words or actions. Finally, he preaches the false to know the true and prefers what is "foolish" to what is clear and simple.

Recognize the Type of Relationship He Has With Others

Whatever we do, it's never good enough. He knows or does better than others. He does not give any compliments, but always finds the small details that allow him to say that it is not perfect. The manipulator often destroys insidiously and cannot help but criticize. He would like to control everything, but since he can't do that, he shows his power by pointing out the weaknesses or mistakes of others. If we are proud of what we have accomplished, he will find a pretext for belittling us and devaluing us. When a parent adopts this type of behavior with his child (or a leader with his employee), he destroys the trust of his victim.

He Is Not Interested in Others

When the manipulator is concerned about any problem, his entire family must be in tune with his emotional state. Wife, husband, or children know that you have to become transparent so as not to attract anger. But everyone also knows that the manipulator always ends up finding a pretext to unload his fury. He's an ego crusher who knows everything better than everyone else. He always has an adventure, a story, or an anecdote more impressive than yours to make you think that you are small, lousy, or uninteresting.

He Is Surrounded By People Who Live in Fear and Failure

At work, with friends or family, we enjoy living in a pleasant atmosphere. Of course, there are times when there is conflict, screaming and arguing, but overall people know how to talk to each other. They trust each other and feel free to live and to do business.

When there is manipulation, the atmosphere is heavy and people do not dare to speak to each other anymore. People isolate themselves in their suffering. Teachers know that when a child becomes isolated and self-contained, they are no longer involved in class and communicate with difficulty. This is a sign that something serious is happening (usually related to the abuse).

In the world of work, one can be certain of the presence of a manipulator from certain symptoms:

- People feel wrong

- The atmosphere is thick and heavy

- There is a lot of absenteeism and sick leave

- The new employees do not stay, and the old ones try to leave

- There are a lot of rumors and gossip

- People watch each other, are jealous of each other, and accuse each other

- People feel more or less strongly because of a lack of direction

- Decisions seem to be made on an ad hoc basis

- Promises are not kept

- Clans form and clash

- Work results drop or remain desperately low

- The staff is de-motivated and no longer believes in anything

- Projects rarely or hardly succeed

To impose his power and knowledge, the manipulator removes what works well and imposes complex and "silly things" that work poorly or which greatly disrupt the activity of all. He invests his energy in vain enterprises, and he frequently gives unjustified reproaches. He gives his opinion on everything and makes others doubt themselves by saying "nonsense" with the utmost confidence.

More insidiously, the manipulator relies on the ignorance or lack of experience of others to better establish his superiority, thanks to these types of remarks: "You'll see when you get to my age... When you have proven yourself, you will be able to speak..."

Henri belongs to this category of characters. As soon as he arrives in his new position, he begins by suppressing all that his predecessor had accomplished and introduces complicated rules that have no reason to exist. He regards any remark or comment as a personal attack. To maintain his authority, he divides and reigns. Thus, when he is alone with Paul, he criticizes what Pierre has been doing for 12 years. As soon as he is with Pierre, he lets the latter hear what he thinks of Paul, who has just left school. Then he lets them fight.

Remember

A manipulator likes to diminish, belittle, and criticize others who generally live in fear and failure. He sows disorder and is only interested in himself. All this implies that he lives surrounded by sad people, worried and in poor health.

He Is a Liar, Cheater, and a Dishonest Person

But he does it with so much self-confidence and naturalness that it's hard to believe it. He is able to contradict himself or to disavow what he has just said a few minutes ago. He also uses the art of slander with a rare mastery.

To accuse a department head that he could not bear, the hospital director said to the board of directors that this person had committed an incalculable number of professional mistakes. His perversity was so felt by all that no one ever dared to ask him for evidence. The fear was such that everyone thought only of protecting themselves and nobody ever dared to challenge or simply contradict him.

He Abuses His Authority

The manipulator has great difficulty in respecting the rules he himself imposes on others. In his capacity as a leader, he imposes procedures that he does not respect himself. Some abuse their authority for perverse purposes like some priests, teachers, or educators accused of pedophilia. These are real manipulators.

He Is Stubborn

His experience is the only valid one and his judgments are without appeal. He says he is always overworked, but on closer inspection, we see that his incompetence, his lack of organization, and his desire to control everything (by refusing to delegate) make him drown in a glass of water.

When something is wrong, a normal person takes a step back to analyze the situation and find a solution. Conversely, the manipulator is unable to recognize his mistakes and change his strategy. This explains why, when he encounters a difficulty, he always blames others for what is happening and then remakes, but on a larger scale, the same mistakes that led him into a deadlock. It turns out that he refuses to confess his mistakes and reveals that he is unable to change.

He cannot tolerate helping those he seeks to weaken, let alone admit to questioning himself. By virtue of the old principle that "the friends of my enemies are my enemies", he wants his victims to remain weak and will attack those who seek to help them.

For the manipulator, help is nothing more than a means to manipulate others better. That's why he interprets any attempt to help him as a personal attack to manipulate him. Not knowing how to manipulate others and especially not wanting to be himself, he cannot accept being wrong and, as a result, will be unable to change anything in his ways of doing and being. Only a balanced person can recognize his mistakes and sincerely change his attitude when necessary. Unfortunately, the manipulator is incapable of it.

Remember

The manipulator is a cheat, a liar, and a dishonest person. He does not abide by his own rules and easily grapples. He recognizes no error, refuses to be wrong or to be helped, and is unable to change.

He Is Obsessed With the Need to Control Everything

A sensible and well-balanced individual exercises good control over himself, his family, his entourage, or his work. He is also quite capable of receiving orders. Conversely, a manipulator has a hard time complying with the constraints others place on him (even if they are simple, like to arrive at work on time).

He Uses His Power to Destroy What Works

As soon as he has a little authority, the manipulator exercises it in a tyrannical and abusive way. A characteristic fact is that he likes to surround himself with incompetent people. It may sound weird, but it does not work that way for no reason. By rewarding those who work poorly, he ensures allies who are very dedicated to him because, without him, they would be nothing. In addition, he can use these people as fuses that he will light at leisure, as soon as a problem may threaten or directly question.

The network of incompetence and dependence he creates around him forms a wall behind which he hides to continue to manipulate with impunity. It can destroy a service, a company, or an administration without anyone realizing it because whatever happens, it is never his fault and always that of others!

Another classic result of this way of doing things is that the best are disgusted by such a mode of operation. They leave or ask to leave when they realize the futility of their efforts and as soon as they understand that their skills will serve them better elsewhere. This backward selection is entirely appropriate for the manipulator and signifies his presence because competence represents for him a real threat (with regard to his own incompetence and that of his protégés).

He Abuses His Power

When a manipulator is authoritarian, it is because he is inefficient or incompetent. We can observe that when he asks for an opinion, it is very often because he does not have one. In the same way, he is very adept at grabbing the work or ideas of others, for example by putting his signature at the bottom of the projects he has commissioned.

Under normal working conditions, it is natural for a manager to benefit from the work of his staff. But if he wants to continue running his service or his business, he will have to know how to reward their efforts. On the other hand, it is abnormal and unhealthy for a manager to steal their employee's work by appropriating it unduly.

He uses his legitimate power to harass or enslave. Whether it is a hierarchical authority or parental authority, as soon as a manipulator has a little power, he will use it to dominate others. One could thus give a thousand and one examples of abuse of power. Among these is the teacher who ridicules a student extensively in front of the whole class. It makes others laugh, but the teacher does not realize how serious it is for a child to suffer such vexations from someone who embodies authority and knowledge. Many school failures have their roots in such situations.

The manipulative parent always seems to act out of love or in the name of the safety of his family, but in reality, he deprives the child of any real possibility of gaining independence. He may also consider the adolescent's desire for autonomy illegitimate.

When Thomas asks his parents for permission to go to a friend's house for a weekend, his mother replies, "What about us? What are we going to do?" For the same reasons, when he is old enough to protect them, he will be prevented from doing odd jobs that could have allowed him to make some pocket money and thus acquire a little autonomy. In the world of work, examples of manipulation using power are common. It would even seem that as soon as a person has some power, they use it to dominate or crush others. Fortunately, there are people who act with a sense of ethics which leads them not to consider themselves superior but, on the contrary, to think that the role of a manager is (as the name suggests) to bring "answers".

A woman, a department head, was very attached to the motivation and spirit of the staff of her unit. The objectives were regularly met, and the staff was very satisfied with the consideration and attention they received. Instead of congratulating himself on these results, the direct supervisor of this department manager took offense at this success and set about systematically destroying the work that this woman had taken years to complete. With contradictory orders and arbitrary decisions, he emptied the workplace and distributed a large part of the staff in other departments. By imaginary and unfounded faults, he removed all the responsibilities from the department head to give them to his subordinates.

Deprived of telephone and computer and having no staff to supervise nor real work to perform, the department head went to see the director-general who listened and made a list of her grievances before asking her:

"What color are the walls of my office?"

- White.

"Well, I tell you they are black, and you must understand that if your leader says they are black, they are black. It's like that! You can try to complain, but you will be crushed. You are not strong enough to fight an administration. This is the earthen pot against the iron pot."

He Is Skilled at Turning Situations to His Advantage

If ever he is suspected, he becomes a victim and accuses others of openly doing what he was trying to do to them underhandedly. If he is (rightly) accused of favoring rumors or mounting people against each other, he is indignant and accuses others of trying to plot against him. This way of proceeding is also a clear sign of the active presence of a manipulator.

If you lend him something, be it a book, a piece of furniture, a car, or even an apartment, you will have a hard time getting it back. If, after many unsuccessful requests, you become impatient, he will eventually accuse you of persecuting him. It is not unheard of that he even goes so far as to sue his benefactor when he simply wants to recover the property or the money that belongs to him.

Manipulators are also very adept at turning back the attacks they endure, considering them a type of persecution. This allows them to assume the role of victim and to affirm that they are in their right. The others then become ignorant or enemies. Under these conditions, any attack directed against a manipulator represents the proof that they are right.

Remember

The manipulator has a haunting need to control everything. He uses or abuses his power to destroy what works, enslave others, or harass them. He knows how to turn situations to his advantage.

Recognize Him in the Environment

It is not always easy to distinguish a manipulator at first glance. He has no horns on his head or fork in his hand. On the other hand, his maneuvers generate signs that mark his presence as surely as the fall of the leaves announces the arrival of autumn.

The Morale of His Entourage Is Low

It is two o'clock in the morning, and Jerome still does not sleep; he fidgets, turns around constantly, remains quiet for a few moments, then, exasperated, he turns on the light and sits on his bed, wondering why he cannot fall asleep. He thinks, closes his eyes and begins to project the film of his day on the screen of his eyelids.

Everything had started well. He had received a nice message from his girlfriend, to whom he was quick to answer. Then there was this interview with his head of lab who had congratulated him for his new project. The rest of the time, he had worked to get things done, before going to the restaurant where he had an appointment with his father.

By early afternoon, back at his office, he had struggled to keep his eyes open and had felt unusually heavy and tired. He thought that it must be some temporary fatigue related to eating such a rich meal. Still pursuing his work, he irretrievably deleted an important file on his computer. He was annoyed because he spent the rest of the day trying to recover data that he could not find and ended up leaving work earlier than planned. And now he cannot sleep and thought, "It looks like it's always like that, as soon as something succeeds, I have to pay for it by having a problem or feeling bad."

In thinking this, Jerome was not far from the truth. But the cause of his sudden and inexplicable fatigue (as well as the mistakes that followed) was not what he had eaten, but the character with whom he had eaten.

To win the approval and recognition of his father, Jerome had told him about his project. His father then said, "That's good, but you're just doing your job. You are paid for it and there is no reason to boast about it. Here, when I was working, I discovered how to reduce the time it took to check parts while maintaining the same quality of work. At that moment, at least, I had hit a serious bonus. But that's good, you do a good job! You just have to keep making efforts. Besides, your project reminds me of the one I performed when I was at home... I will explain to you..." Then follows an interminable speech of the father on his past exploits.

A witness in this conversation might have thought that the father was approving his son and was trying to give him advice. But in reality, the father's speech was intended to minimize Jerome's success and diminish the value of his efforts.

Since his childhood, Jerome had suffered the harmful influence of a father who wanted to prove his superiority by preventing his son from exceeding him, all while inviting him to do so. In these conditions, it is not surprising that Jerome prevents himself from succeeding or is always attracted to problems as soon as he begins to succeed.

The unconscious message of the father is still there, in his head, which says to him: "Try to exceed me, but you will not be able to succeed in doing so." A certain tension is always there in his presence, we feel compelled to adopt attitudes that do not suit us. But on the contrary, as soon as he is no longer there, we feel much freer.

It was only once alone, on holiday with his young son, that Edwige heard him laugh out loud. It was the first time they had let themselves play together like crazy. It was a shock to her because she realized that this never happened in the presence of her husband: "I had never realized, until this day, how intimidating his presence was and how it prevented us from having fun naturally, as a mother does with her child. When my husband is here, you must always be serious. It's sinister!"

In some offices or workshops, we can notice that the atmosphere suddenly becomes much more relaxed as soon as a specific person is absent or goes on leave. If our morale evolves into a jagged one, with inexplicable drops and upsets of tone, it is likely that, in one way or another, we are in contact with a manipulator. Sudden changes in morale (with sudden moments of depression followed, in the more or less long-term, euphoric upsurges preceding the next collapse), are obvious symptoms of harassment or type III manipulation.

He Can Destroy by Pretending to Help

When some nineteenth-century missionaries arrived in a village or were confronted with people to convert, they began by destroying all elements of indigenous culture to impose theirs better. A little later, and in the same way, some teachers succeeded in imposing the French language by punishing children who spoke another language at school. They forced them to wear a rusty hoof or nail tied around their necks when they let themselves speak their mother tongue at school.

Claude is head of the department. He is also responsible for the ongoing training of staff. Regularly, he receives the employees and approaches, at each interview, a particular technical subject. In the week following this training, he masks his voice and telephones the employees, pretending to be an external client who is always very difficult to satisfy. Then, referring to the alleged complaint of a client, he summons the agents who gave the wrong answers and verbally berates them until he makes them cry.

Guilt in the Air

In the wake of the manipulator, we breathe air that is made stale by the ambient guilt. Thus, the manipulator lives surrounded by characters (whether family members or co-workers) accustomed to evolving "bent" under the weight of their deep sense of guilt.

This last point is really terrible because, in addition to being manipulated, the victims feel responsible and, most often, guilty of what happens to them. The manipulator makes them feel guilty by giving advice afterward: "You should have suspected... You should have paid more attention... Everyone knows that..." If a problem arises and even if he is at fault, he will make sure that you feel responsible. If he spanks his son or leaves his wife, he will say, "It was you who forced me to do it." In reality, his son may have done something wrong and his wife may have done something wrong, but the former never asked his father to be violent and the second never forced her husband to pick a mistress and leave with her.

The manipulator makes his victim feel guilty in order to deflect suspicion and render the victim incapable of defending himself. This is the case for almost all incest victims who feel deeply guilty for what they have suffered. There are also many battered women who resign themselves to hell because they mistakenly think they deserve it.

This sense of well-deserved punishment is also present in almost all victims of rape, assault, or accident. For years, they seek to understand how they are responsible for what happened to them. Sometimes it is better to have a bad answer when you feel guilty than to remain ignorant and doubtful. It is on this ambiguity that the manipulator plays to make his victims feel guilty.

To make others feel guilty and especially to avoid feeling guilty himself, the manipulator exploits, in a perverse way, the ideas generally accepted by society. So, he uses a non-exhaustive list of common phrases:

- If it is not done well, it is badly done.

- One must be competent in all circumstances.

- People complain, but it's often their fault.

- Between friends, we can say everything; when we do you a favor, we must know how to render it otherwise.

- There are only fools who do not change their minds.

It is not the expressions that are important, but the intention of the one who uses them.

Stéphane realized the dream of his life by buying a small bookstore in the province. To help him, he brings in a former colleague. At first, they coexist in the euphoria of the installation. There is everything to do and morale is good.

Stéphane quickly becomes overwhelmed by the doubts and worries that beset him. He has the impression that he will never succeed and that he is not up to it.

It was only years later that he realized how his former colleague had aggravated problems and regularly sabotaged his efforts and then gently encouraged him to find in himself what he might have missed.

It is because the manipulator knows how to make us so guilty that we dare not refuse him the money, the service, the object, or the effort that he asks us.

Remember

The manipulator exhausts the energy of those around him or approaching him. He generates tension and the people around him have a high morale that goes down incomprehensibly when he arrives. He can destroy someone by pretending to help him. He acts in such a way that his victims feel guilty for what he does to them.

Chapter 3 - Test Your Confidence

Faced with some people, we sometimes feel embarrassment, doubt or experience repulsion (more or less sudden) that is unexplained. Often, these warning signals are not taken into account, and there is a tendency to look down on or even feel guilty about having such ideas. One then castigates himself while repeating to himself:

- One must not see evil everywhere.

- You do not judge someone until you know them.

- You always have to trust.

- Do not be paranoid.

- It is not appropriate to have such thoughts.

- Give him a chance...

As long as we have the naivety to see and think of the other person in our image, we give manipulators the freedom to abuse us. We are like sheep who think that all other animals are vegetarians like them. The day a wolf comes to the door of the sheepfold proclaiming his hunger, the sheep opens the door and invites him to enter to share his meal. To avoid this type of error, we have developed a test that allows us to uncover the true personality of the person who cannot be identified or whose sincerity is questioned. This is the confidence test that identifies a manipulator on the basis of his actions and not accusing him of arbitrary judgments, ideas, or rumors.

We all have our share of shade and our share of light. When we fall in love, we only see what draws us to the other: his smile, his intelligence, his eyes, his body, his voice, his sense of humor, etc. We only take into account the good sides of the person who attracts us. But when we separate or when we divorce, we only see his bad sides.

Reality is not always what we believe; no one is entirely an angel or entirely a demon. It is for this reason that each line of the confidence test is made of two questions highlighting the good and bad sides of the one we suspect of manipulation.

A single coin always has two faces that are impossible to see at the same time. To help us get away from the doubt and out of the confusion, each line of the trust test alternately draws our attention to the positive side and then to the negative side of the same behavior. After answering all the questions and considering the difference between the positive results and the negative results, the final result reveals the reliability or, on the contrary, the more or less manipulative aspect of the person thus evaluated.

The Test of Confidence

To defend oneself well, it is necessary to know who attacks us and how we are attacked.

Communication

1. He holds endless and fuzzy speeches. He actively opposes the spread of rumors.

2. He loves to gossip. He does not dwell on bad news.

3. He speaks in generalities. He communicates the facts without distorting them.

4. He blocks communication and preaches falsehoods as if they were true. He is attentive to the problems of others.

5. He knows everything, and it is very difficult to impress him. He clearly indicates the origin of his information.

6. He uses others to spread his messages. He avoids hurting people.

7. He devalues and belittles others. He knows how to keep a secret and will not betray others.

8. He does not keep his promises. He recognizes his limits and tries to exceed them.

9. He cannot think of being wrong and refuses to change. He is

fundamentally honest.

Relational

10. He surrounded himself with people living in fear and failure and brings order where there isn't. He is a positive influence on those he associates with.

11. He creates suspicion and sows discord. He enriches the understanding or knowledge of his audience.

12. He displays a disconcerting assurance or crushes others. He is the target of those who have things to hide.

13. He seems harmless, even very friendly. He knows how to pass the sponge easily.

14. He is very resentful and does not forgive anything. He respects the time and efforts of others.

15. He waits for the last moment to act or ask. He loves and promotes teamwork.

16. He divides and reigns. He brings support and comfort.

17. He can destroy someone by pretending to help him. He energizes and makes you want to surpass yourself.

18. He exhausts the energies of those who approach him. He values and encourages his entourage.

19. He is surrounded by people who are often sick or absent. He

inspires those around him to work hard and improve.

How to Use the Confidence Test

To unravel the reality of appearances, you must first read the two propositions of each line before deciding which one best fits your idea. This alternative makes it possible to provide correctly measured answers for each line of the test.

Do not answer all questions in one column before moving on to another. This would undermine the impartiality of our judgment by only amplifying the defects of those who annoy us and embellish blindly the reality of those we appreciate. Again, it is imperative to evaluate the positive and negative aspects of each behavior before moving on to the next.

It may happen that the person exhibits characteristics of both propositions on the line. In this case, check both the positive and negative sides.

After answering all the questions, simply add the results of each column to find out how much and which side tilts the balance of that personality. The result will be positive if the person is reliable and negative if the person turns out to be manipulative.

It is possible to refine the analysis by studying the distribution of crosses more closely. This allows one to see if the person is reliable or a manipulator in what he says (communication) and in what he is (relational). For example, a person can be very reliable in his activities but manipulative in his communication.

Thus, a very professional person communicates in a clear, concise, and precise way with the customers. But when she is with her colleagues, she speaks only by innuendo and likes to circulate rumors to pit people against each other.

If you cannot answer the confidence test questions, there is a good chance that this is because of the confusion caused by the behavior of the manipulator who changes his attitude according to the circumstances or situations he is in. To study these cases, consider determining a specific area of analysis before answering the test questions and keep in mind some examples of suspicious areas: with clients, with colleagues, when you are alone with him, with your family, with friends...

The Results of the Confidence Test

The Result Is Negative

From 0 to -5: Suspicion! We must continue to monitor this person and to avoid giving anything important to him before obtaining confirmation of his real attitude and before knowing, with certainty, in what areas we can or cannot trust him.

From -5 to -10: Be vigilant! This kind of individual is currently unreliable. It is imperative to control what he says and does in a rigorous and accurate setting. As far as possible, constraints must be imposed to limit the extent of the problems.

From -10 to -15: Attention! He is certainly a manipulator. You have to know how to say no and do not let yourself be lulled by his words. Do not hesitate to ask him for clarification and to verify his statements. Avoid staying too long in his presence.

From -15 to -20: Danger! For sure, he is a very dangerous manipulator. Do not be fooled by threats or promises. Gather written evidence before considering attacking it head-on. If possible, do not go out to meet him or stay in prolonged contact with this person. If this is not possible, avoid talking about sensitive topics. Do like the English, speak exclusively of the weather and leave as soon as possible.

From -20 to -30: Great danger! This kind of manipulator extremely destructive and perverse. However, they are fortunately very rare (Hitler, Stalin or Saddam Hussein). If he has some power, he will be very difficult to defeat. Before doing anything, read the last two chapters of this book very carefully. In the meantime, avoid him without running away. If you cannot, stay polite and get out of reach quickly.

The Result Is Positive

From 0 to 5: Stay wary! We must continue to monitor this person and especially avoid giving anything important to him before we are more certain about him and know what situations he is reliable in and which he is not.

From 5 to 10: Caution! We are dealing here with moderately reliable behavior. It is better to avoid trusting him too much before he has proven himself and you are sure of him.

From 10 to 15: Good result! He is a reliable person to trust and rely on. You should recognize his qualities and tell him.

From 15 to 20: Excellent! This individual is extremely reliable and competent. They are a precious person with whom one can work and live with confidence.

From 20 to 30: Miracle! This kind of person is, unfortunately, a very rare jewel. Keep your relationship with them carefully and above all, be very careful not to lose it.

Chapter 4 - The Four Kinds of Manipulators

By reading the confidence test for the first time, some readers may recognize themselves and think that they themselves are manipulators. This reflex is, after all, quite natural because, at one time or another, and for some reason, we have all been led to act by manipulation. What mother has never said to her child, "Eat your mashed potatoes to please Mum"? Who has never lied about his resume or his qualities to get a job or a simple appointment? Who has never asked someone for something or service when he could have done it on his own?

As long as these manipulations remain occasional, it does not make us real manipulators. In the same way that you can have a camera and make holiday movies without being a professional filmmaker, you can occasionally practice manipulation without really being a manipulator. Unlike the occasional manipulator, the professional manipulator constantly uses others to his advantage. He regularly uses trickery or blackmail to achieve his ends, or he tirelessly needs to crush others to feel powerful.

Before tackling such manipulation specialists, one must be able to distinguish them from an occasional manipulator. This will save us from killing a mosquito with a hammer or attacking a tiger with a fly swatter.

To better abuse his victims, the manipulator uses various disguises. There are four types of manipulators:

- The charming manipulator

- The manipulative manipulator

- The respectable manipulator

- The authoritarian manipulator

Knowing and understanding what is hidden behind each of these four masks is essential to avoid falling into the traps they hold out for us.

The Charming Manipulator

In old tales, a spell was the magical means unscrupulous individuals used to achieve their ends. In the same way and in everyday life, there are manipulators who use a charm or who abuse a natural sympathy to deceive their victims.

It is difficult to refuse something to someone nice or someone who makes a request with a bright smile. Even if one feels, in the depths of oneself, that one should not do it, one often ends up yielding because he knows how to be nice, he speaks with ease and seems attentive to the others. It is not because he is a manipulator that he has no qualities. On the contrary, this type of manipulator uses his qualities to be appreciated and better conceal his maneuvers under a facade that is quite acceptable, even pleasant.

We have already seen that a good salesman (type II manipulator) knew how to be friendly in different ways. Intuitively or by dint of learning, he finds in his clients the form of sympathy that suits them. This allows him to naturally come in contact with them and create a favorable climate to get them to buy what he offers them often without them thinking of refusing.

At work, with friends or in everyday life, it is not always easy to realize that you are in the presence of a manipulator and sometimes you have to work with him for a while before realizing it.

One of the main reasons for this difficulty comes from the fact that the victims of charming manipulators are people who more or less tend to repress or deny their own aspirations. For various reasons (including fear of displeasing others), they are more attentive to meeting the needs of others than to fulfill their personal desires.

Thus, even when they think it very hard, it is sometimes very difficult for them to say no to someone who solicits them nicely.

This mother-in-law arrives at her children's home to relieve her daughter-in-law, who has just given birth. Elie immediately takes the house in hand. She does everything, takes care of everything, but in her own way. As a result, even if her services were appreciated at first, the young parents now feel overwhelmed by her presence. Mother-in-law crushes her children and prevents them from living. They no longer feel like they are home and would like to be alone, but they do not know how to tell her that she is getting too cumbersome. They console themselves by saying: "She is so nice that you cannot refuse to let her stay. It makes her so happy."

The victims of charming manipulators tend to model their attitude on that of others or let them choose in their place ("I do not know me, do what you want, I'll let you choose").

This type of attitude (it is mainly about submission) then leaves all the freedom to the charming manipulator to seduce his victim and obtain from her what he wants. How many girls have been seduced and then abandoned without care. We often blame ourselves for having been duped, to have given in or to have been unable to resist, but it is always too late to react. The charming manipulator is often a seducer who perfectly handles the art of flattery or fascination. He never gives anything in exchange, or he does the bare minimum to appease her desires, reassure her and, ultimately, achieve his goal.

This concern for the economy has fascinated the famous criminal Landru. After seducing his future victims with fine speeches and tender words, then making sure of their small fortune, he proposed that they should visit his suburban house.

However, instead of buying two "back and forth" tickets, as most would Landru, took only one for him and a "one way" for the other who would never come back because he knew that he was going to kill her and make her disappear.

It's not because a person is friendly that you have to be wary of thinking that he is a manipulator. Most friendly people have no ulterior motives. On the other hand, it would be just as imprudent to believe that someone friendly is unable to harm us.

The Manipulative Manipulator

If some manipulators play on superficiality or on the weakness of their victims, others rely on the feeling of unease that we experience every time we take or receive something without giving anything in exchange. They exploit what is called, in social psychology, the principle of reciprocity.

This principle is socially inscribed in us, and we can thus formulate it: "If I am given something, I must absolutely give something else in exchange." It is especially by virtue of this principle that one does not go to someone's house empty-handed when one is invited. Whoever does not obey this principle experiences a feeling of embarrassment, guilt or shame, as a result of the education he has received from social interactions.

The method adopted by the manipulative manipulator plays on this principle. The latter uses the principle of reciprocity according to a very precise method:

- First, he begins by giving or recalling that he has given something important to us.

- Then, he imposes on us the idea that we have a debt to him and takes advantage of it to ask us, in exchange, for something disproportionate.

- Finally, by playing on the guilt generated by the principle of reciprocity, he makes us unable to refuse what he asks.

If the manipulator pays us a few euros and even if we return them quickly, he will use this loan to ask us one day to loan him a large sum because it is he who sets the time and method to pay this moral debt.

If he happens once to transport us in his car, he will not hesitate, when the time comes, to ask us (in exchange) to lend him our vehicle for a week telling us, "When you did not have a car, I did not hesitate to help you out. So now that it's my turn, you can give me this little service!"

Serious Consequences

After reading his son's academic results, a manipulative parent tries to convince his child of the need to change his behavior:

"We bled to the veins so that you could go to school, we did everything for you, and that's how you thank us! Are you not ashamed of doing us so much harm? You are only an egoist, you only think of yourself, you make fun of us, and you should be ashamed. If you do not put more effort into your work, you will not achieve anything. "

By dint of hearing this kind of speech and living in this guilt-ridden atmosphere, the child has developed an unconscious reflex which prevents him from being happy and causes him to do poorly at the things he undertakes to continue to give reason to his parents unconsciously. The consequences of emotional manipulation are "hard" and difficult to erase, but it is often enough to be clearly aware of it to be released.

All manipulations are really dangerous only as long as we remain ignorant of the mechanisms put in place or that we are mistaken. The manipulative manipulator also sometimes plays on the diffuse feeling of the victim of having committed a fault or having a debt to pay.

Madeleine never married and remained in the service of her parents all her life because she thought she was indebted to them for all the efforts they had made for her. It took her a long time to discover that her parents were content to play their part. There was no objective reason for her to feel indebted and sacrifice her adult life.

Family manipulations are not the easiest to perceive and fight. The closeness of people, the complexity of relationships, and the multitude of situations are elements that often prevent the perception of reality.

To foil the plans of a manipulative manipulator, one must first correctly evaluate what he has given us to make a comparison with what he wishes to receive in exchange. If the two are not proportionate, there is no legitimate reciprocity and therefore no reason to feel guilty for not meeting his request. We are then much more free and willing to discuss, argue, and refuse what he claims he should receive.

The Respectable Manipulator

This kind of manipulator adopts a behavior (the presence, the charisma) that imposes respect and which induces a form of submission to the perceived knowledge and authority. This reflex (of submission) makes us attentive and benevolent with respect to everything that embodies knowledge or authority.

From early childhood, we were taught to respect adults and not to speak without permission. At school, we were made to understand that we had to obey the teacher, listen to him, and keep quiet in class. When you are an adult, you listen to your boss, follow the advice of your notary and your banker or those of a cardiologist, without even questioning their honesty or competence. On the other hand, one would be wary more spontaneously of a mechanic, a plumber, or a car salesman. Many financial scams rely on this reflex of submission to respectability and knowledge.

We maintain a veritable reflex of submission, and the respectable manipulator likes to feel his superiority by playing on this natural tendency to submit to authority. He will abuse his titles, his diplomas, his experience, his money, his property, his relations, his past, or simply the aura that confers his craft to crush the other. At his touch, we have the unpleasant sensation of feeling lousy, uneducated, ignorant, or completely stupid. This is also the goal because the respectable manipulator does not trust his target and uses others to assert his superiority. This is how he often has a slightly contemptuous attitude which marks him as different.

Faced with a grandson who accuses him of being a manipulator, a grandmother replies: "We do not talk to our grandmother this way, and first of all, you owe me respect!" If the word "grandmother" had been replaced by "husband", "wife", or "friend," the manipulation would have been the same.

These manipulators who advance masked behind what they think to be the attributes of respectability have, in reality, a great need for the admiration of others to exist. Without them, that is to say without us, and especially without our admiration or desire to look like them, their manipulations would not work anymore, and they would not represent anything.

However, is respectability harmful, and must we systematically be wary of those who impress us?

Contrary to what the respectable manipulator suggests to us, respect is not something that should be demanded, but something that should be deserved.

It is not difficult to identify a truly respectable person. When one is in their presence, one has the feeling of being more alive, of existing more. Becoming more intelligent, one has the impression that they will learn and grow spiritually or intellectually.

The Authoritarian Manipulator

This one is very easily identifiable, because of the fear or even the terror he inspires. The authoritarian manipulator is indeed convinced that to succeed in professional, political, social or family life, it is necessary to impose oneself by force. For him, to be strong is to be inflexible, not to show his feelings, and even less to take into account those of others.

The authoritarian manipulator is usually someone who is hard on himself and hard on others. He does not know how to give compliments and does not waste his time in preliminaries. He goes straight to the point because for him, only the result counts. He (she) thinks that one should always prefer efficiency to feelings. Conviviality or affectionate exchanges represent a waste of time. The authoritarian manipulator is convinced that the whole world is selfish and does not care about the fate of others. What others feel or do with their lives does not interest him at all.

The authoritarian manipulator imposes and demands. He is often unpleasant, and when he needs service, he loses neither his time nor his energy to seduce or convince. He does not have the motivation and all that stuff. The only strategy he knows is that of uncompromising order, threats, and punishment. For the same reasons, it will never occur to him to thank or congratulate those who obey him. Words to say he likes you or thank you are not part of his vocabulary. He knows only criticism.

The authoritarian manipulator thinks that the world does not pity the weak and that showing his feelings is an unacceptable weakness. That's why his emotions are buried in the depths of his body as if they were something incongruous and shameful. It is often said of him that he has no heart. He remains indifferent to the love of others. For him, what counts above all is to ensure control of the situation by being feared and respected.

Louis XIV, who wanted at all costs to avoid plots, controlled the nobles of his court through "etiquette". The latter was a long list of everything that was allowed or forbidden. He reached the heights of manipulation by taking the name of Sun King because he displayed an authority and power at least equal to those of the star of the day that allows life and cannot be seen head-on without becoming blind.

The authoritarian manipulator thinks that authority is the supreme value that makes the world work. However, he may reproach you for being selfish and heartless if he finds that you are not taking enough care of him. In his novel *Viper in the Fist*, Hervé Bazin remarkably describes his childhood suffering caused by a manipulative and authoritarian mother he had dubbed Folcoche.

When the manipulator is particularly violent, one forgets the manipulative aspects to remember only his attitude that one will be happy to describe as choleric or temperamental. Yet it is always manipulation because it seeks to get something by playing on the fear of the other.

Take a director who is constantly "on the back" of his staff to the point that he overwhelms them with procedures and guidelines to better control them. He punishes the slightest error with the utmost severity and does not give any freedom of conduct. Like a Ceausescu or Saddam Hussein before the fall, he arbitrarily imposes his principles without worrying about the consequences. He directs, orders, and punishes with all his might. Thanks to this policy of unfailing terror (which silences everyone), no one moves or dares to complain about the fear of being the next victim. From the outside, the establishment seems to work quite properly, and if you do not look too closely, everything seems to aim for the best in the best of all worlds.

The authoritarian manipulator likes and chooses professions or command posts in relation to his taste for power and control. In the private sector, his partners are dull and subject to his will, unless they are even more authoritarian than him. Such as this German teacher from a sad memory who covered his students with screams and insults concerning a minor grammatical mistake, but who operated the classroom smoothly before his wife when she was at his side.

Chapter 5 - How to Handle Manipulators

Egocentric manipulators (type II) are sad characters who abuse our kindness, our ignorance, or one of our weaknesses to extort something from us. They are not necessarily malicious toward us, but when they want something, they are ready to do anything to get it (and it does not matter what it can cost us).

How can we avoid being forced to do their will? How should we behave and what should we answer when we are asked for a service that we do not want to return? In a word, how can we escape this form of manipulation?

All of this is relatively simple and consists of four points. To resist a type II manipulator one must:

- Know that manipulation exists.

- Take a step back to observe and understand what is happening to us.

- Mourn an ideal world.

- Learn to spot the intent of the manipulator.

Be Aware of Their Existence

There are people with their "head in the air", who are naive or candid and, trusting the good looks of those they meet, systematically trust everyone. Needless to say, all these gentle dreamers are ideal prey for manipulators.

Knowing or remembering that manipulation exists is an essential first step because the most dangerous manipulation is the one we do not see. This does not mean that you have to be wary of everything and everyone. Leave that to the paranoid! It is simply necessary to remain attentive and not to neglect our instinctive reactions. The feeling of uneasiness we feel and the doubt that surrounds us in the presence of certain people or projects are all small warning signs that must arouse our distrust.

When Virginie told Baptiste of his desire to set up a business to exploit an original idea for embroidery, he found the idea inspiring. A few months later, Virginie asked him to join the project financially. Baptiste then felt a strange sensation which knotted his stomach and which incited him not to engage. He felt a bit guilty about not helping his friend, but he quickly silenced his scruples by accusing himself of being too selfish and thinking only of money. Finally, focused on the originality of the project, he committed himself for a rather large sum. Unfortunately, Virginia quickly went bankrupt because she did not know how to manage, did not listen to anyone, and did not do as she should. Naturally, Baptiste never saw his money again.

Remember

Manipulation exists, but our intuition or warning signals are there to warn us of possible danger. They recommend that we be more attentive and be wary of going further.

Knowing How to Take a Step Back

Taking a step back means being able to observe what is going on without *a priori* and without ready-made ideas. This attitude is the only one that allows a fairer view of events because we must not forget that the danger of the manipulator is precisely his ability to convince us of the reality of his character. All his art is to make us believe in the image of him that he wants to give us.

Manipulation is a fragile construction that collapses as soon as it is revealed. This is why the manipulator does everything in his power to prevent us from taking a step back and allowing us to think. He would risk being unmasked and get lost.

To take a step back is also to refuse to commit too quickly. It knows how to ask or take time to reflect, to evaluate the commitment that is asked of us and its subsequent consequences. It is reading what is written (in small print) at the bottom of a contract, especially if the salesman tells you that it is not important.

Mourning an Ideal World

It is only when one accepts and sees the reality that one can really start to act effectively. To mourn an ideal communication or an idyllic world is to see things as they are and not as we would like them to be.

We can dream of a world based on trust and mutual respect, of a world in which men are all valued and where there are no arguments, manipulations, or violence. One can also imagine a world without obstacles where courage and effort would be rewarded, a world where honest people would live in peace and where the wicked and the incompetent would cease to harm. We can dream...

But to dream without acting is to flee from reality. Some expressions illustrate this refusal to be confronted with reality in what is harshest or most unpleasant: "This is not normal... It's not possible to be so mean... It should not happen... It's too unfair... How can we see such things, they should not exist..."

Refusing to see what is happening in order to dream up a comfortable and serene imaginary ideal is the surest way to suffer and to be manipulated. It's as safe as driving against traffic on a highway.

If fear does not deter danger, refusing to see it still isn't the best way to avoid it. It's as ridiculous as moving into a minefield, claiming loudly that there is no risk.

Believing that lies, malice, or deceit should not exist is not only an illusion that does not avert danger, but it is also one of the best ways to attract it. To refuse to believe that a person can be a manipulator (when they are) is to increase the risk of becoming a victim.

But beware, seeing things as they do not mean resignation or submission. We can very well see the world as it is and nevertheless work on its evolution without taking refuge in a fake utopia.

If I do not have money, and I do not waste my time dreaming of what I would do if I were rich, I can organize myself to win and improve my situation. In the same way, if I accept my illness instead of lamenting or feeling sorry for the injustice of my fate, I will be able to use all my energy to fight against evil and recover health.

Finally, I will be better able to defend myself, or even to attack, if I accept the sad reality of the frantic ambition of a colleague, the unique yet difficult to tolerate member of my family or, more generally, the unbearable aspect of this or that situation.

Whoever agrees to find that he is being manipulated (without wasting time whining or crying over his fate), can organize himself to defend himself and act. The one who constantly dreams of a better world cannot properly understand his environment, and it is not surprising that he continues to be manipulated and suffer.

Sylvie could not accept the separation from her companion. She was sure he was coming back. They were so made for each other, it was not possible otherwise, she was sure! The more weeks and months passed, the more she sank into her dream: an impossible and eternal love. This was her only topic of conversation. She talked about it to everyone and used even the slightest pretext to talk about this love that could not disappear in this way.

On two or three occasions, she crossed the paths of men in love with her, but, hypnotized by her dream, she did not realize it. It was only years later that she realized that her dream had been a carefully maintained nightmare of not seeing abandonment, rupture, and rejection in the face. From this observation, she was able to put an end to her suffering and even smile at her past mistakes. Having accepted and faced reality, she was able to start a new life, happier and more peaceful.

Remember

Mourning a missed communication or an ideal world is seeing things the way they are. It is closing the door to the suffering that slips between what is and what we would like it to be. It is to be able to face the difficulties and pitfalls of existence with courage and efficiency.

Knowing How to Spot the Intention of the Manipulator

To locate a manipulator by being aware of their existence and to take the necessary distance to reveal manipulation through their behavior is not always enough to understand their intent. There are manipulations "with drawers" so subtle and twisted that it is almost impossible to guess the intention of the manipulator. It is the application of a principle known to all: one manipulation can hide another.

Movies like "The Scam" or "The Cellar Rebound" work according to this principle. The main character deceives both the police and his acolytes into believing that his manipulation has failed. In reality, this failure will allow him to succeed in a much larger manipulation operation which remained secret to all.

Discovering a hidden purpose requires extensive knowledge of the manipulator and a little imagination. This is not always easy and requires trial and error. When one discovers the intention of a manipulator, while coming out of the fog, one feels like much less of a victim. We can then try to beat the manipulator at his own game or, more simply, counter the manipulation by revealing his real projects.

Chapter 6 - Why Is It Difficult to Resist Manipulators?

A manipulator manages to reach his goal by playing on the weak points of his victims. His flair and experience make him choose those who seem to be the least assertive in life or who are least able to defend themselves. If necessary, he can weaken the resistance of his victims by playing on their fears or their preconceptions.

The Manipulator First Attacks the Weak

The Observation

The weakness is a more or less momentary situation that often comes from an unfavorable balance of power. This is the case, for example, when one is confronted by a disdainful superior, a representative of the order who notices an offense, or a big, threatening man covered with tattoos.

The weakness can also come from a deficient physical state related to illness, fatigue, or overwork. Even if it is momentary, this weakness is none the less real and perceptible by the manipulator.

The weakness can be of psychological origin. Thus, the one who feels inferior, less rich, less intelligent, less beautiful, or less capable than his interlocutor automatically places himself in a position of inferiority and weakness. A decrease in morale or a depressive state weakens the defenses and exposes him more fully to the attacks of the manipulators.

In any case, a state of weakness hinders self-assertion and the ability to defend oneself. This is why we must not let the manipulator take advantage of his superiority, giving him too hastily what he expects.

To Resist

When one feels weak, the solution is simple: you must not be reactive. It is urgent not to rush or make decisions that you will inevitably regret one day or another. As little as possible must be said or done and you must avoid making hasty decisions by postponing what the manipulator asks until later.

When one feels both manipulated, and in a position of weakness, the way to do this is as follows:

- Begin by making the manipulator understand that his claim has been well understood.

- Then insist that one is not able to answer, for the moment, its requirements.

- Finally, finish the conversation as quickly as possible, while remaining polite.

"I understand that what you're asking me is important to you, but for the moment, I cannot answer it. Thank you."

"Thank you for thinking of me by making me the offer, but you see I am not able to make a decision. Goodbye."

"I understand that (reformulate their request), but I cannot. Excuse me." Then, leave as soon as possible!

When one feels weak or inferior, one must not flee shamefully. To do so would be an indicator of weakness that shows the manipulator that he can continue to harass us in peace. What is needed is to leave the interaction by operating a strategic retreat based on the following three actions: acknowledge receipt, defuse, and stop.

Acknowledgment means that we have understood their request. It's a question of being able to formulate it, with our words. This reformulation shows without question that we have fully understood what the manipulator has just told us. It does not allow the manipulator to take advantage of our misunderstanding or to insist heavily. The acknowledgment of receipt must be clear enough to indicate to the manipulator that we have understood what he wanted.

Defusing is simply saying (without getting lost in the details) that we are not in a condition or not able to respond to his request.

To stop is to quickly and politely interrupt conservation, without waiting for other answers. You must intend to stop the conversation without regret or remorse.

In a bar, a client tries to seduce the waitress who brings her order. After a few exchanges, he asks her "What time do you finish tonight?"

- Thank you for looking at my schedules (Acknowledge), but answering you is not part of my job. (Defuse)

- What a pity!

- Thank you, sir, goodbye. (Stop)

A friend (who is a notoriously bad payer) asks you: "I do not know who to ask for money to pay for the repair of my car."

- Yes, I understand, this is not a pleasant situation. (Acknowledge)

- I will pay you back as soon as I have received the money I owe.

- Well, in these conditions, I think you'll get out of it. (Defuse)

- I hope.

- Bye! (Stop)

In operating a strategic retreat, sometimes we just put the problem back so that we don't need to deal with it while we may make a poor decision.

Remember

We cannot win every time! The strategic retreat at least avoids being manipulated once again. Think of a Type II manipulation in which you were in a weak position. Then, just imagine how you could have responded by using the three stages of strategic retreat.

The Manipulator Prefers Liabilities

The Observation

Passive people represent about a third of the people we meet in life. The manipulator appreciates them enormously because they do not allow themselves to react and do not know how to defend themselves; they are victims of choice for him. He finds them very easily and attacks them directly.

Generally, the passive person does not require anything because he is afraid of imposing himself. He prefers to be crushed underfoot rather than to say he is walking on his feet. He may be generous enough not to appear selfish or make disproportionate gifts to redeem imaginary or benign faults.

Passives are very discreet people who do not want to disturb. They are shy people who do not speak much or who spend their time apologizing. They are almost unable to refuse what they are asked for fear of appearing insensitive, antisocial, or unsympathetic. It is very difficult for them to talk about themselves and almost impossible to put themselves first.

They are often excessively helpful because they are more concerned with the interests of others than with their own needs. The problem with liabilities is that they forget their own existence and prefer to submit (forgetting themselves) rather than face conflict, disagreement, or judgment.

Passivity has deep roots that often go back to childhood. This state of affairs won't be easily changed by reading a few lines. However, it is possible to explore a few tracks to help those who tend to behave in this way.

To Resist

To get out of the state of inferiority and loneliness in which he finds himself, the passive must be able to imagine that he is a human being just like others and that his opinion and desires are at least as valid as those men and women around him.

"Basically, all the other people I meet are like me. I am not the only one to suffer. Every man or woman I meet in life has experienced suffering. Everyone runs after happiness and seeks to satisfy his needs. But, at the same time, nobody has lived through the same things as me. No one knows what I live deeply, and no one knows exactly how much I suffer. All of these people are different from me just as I am different from others. My opinions and desires are just as respectable as theirs. There are no superior or inferior people, there are only different people who are all equally respectable."

It is common to compare one aspect or detail of one's life with the same detail, or the same aspect of another's life. One does not hesitate to say that one person is richer, more competent, more muscular, or more famous than another. We can compare cars or bank accounts, but we cannot compare globally between them.

If one evaluates someone in the entirety of their existence, nobody resembles anyone because each experience is different. We all move forward in life with a unique story that determines, to a large extent, the decisions we make at every moment. In these conditions, no one is like anyone, and nobody can compare to anyone. We are as we are, and there is neither shame nor pride in feeling different. We can (and must always) seek to improve, but in the end, we will never be anything but ourselves.

To accept others as they are is still the best way to accept oneself. To better understand all that this covers, here is a little exercise that we can do and redo for as long as we are surrounded.

Observe a person discreetly while repeating to you this series of sentences: "This person is like me, she also knew sorrow, sadness, despair... This person is like me and tries to avoid suffering... This person is like me, she needs to love and be loved... This person is like me and is looking for happiness... This person is like me, there are no two identical people... This person is like me, she is the only one to be who she is."

Repeat with different people until you feel a shift in your perception of others or yourself.

The Manipulator Wakes Up Our Fears

The Observation

When a manipulator attacks someone who is neither weak nor passive, he still has the opportunity to achieve his goals by playing on the fear experienced by his victim. By playing this type of chord, the manipulator prevents the person from asserting himself and undermines his defenses as well as his ability to resist.

One of the uncontrollable fears that make us a designated victim is the fear of being hurt or hurting someone by denying them what they ask for. The manipulator spots wake up and use these kinds of fears to get us to do what he wants without us being able to defend ourselves.

The fear of giving oneself a bad image is blackmail that the manipulator also knows how to use, "Have you thought of what people will say if you ever do that?"

The fear of being judged often forces one to act against one's own desire.

One is also a victim of manipulation when one is afraid of offending the other: "You will not do that to me... You cannot refuse me this service... Listen, do it for me... I understand that you can refuse anyone, but not me... You cannot refuse to do that for your mother... Listen, I'm your friend all the same!"

Some manipulations are based on the fear of disappointing the other: "You know, I really need this money and I can't count on anyone but you... You can not disappoint me it's too serious for me."

Blackmail plays on the fear of losing someone, "If you do not do this for me, you do not love me."

But sometimes it is pride that makes us fall into the trap of manipulation, "You know, I could not ask this of just anyone, and I can only really count on you. I know you'll be discreet, won't you?"

It is very difficult to resist manipulations that play on the heartstrings of esteem, friendship, or love. The feelings we have for the manipulator should not play the role of the tree that hides the forest. It is not what binds us to the manipulator that is important, it is what he asks us or what he forces us to do.

To Resist

To oppose these different types of egocentric manipulations, here is the question that must immediately be asked:

"If someone broke away from me because I did not give in to the blackmail he subjected me to, is that really someone who deserves my affection? On the contrary, is it not (at least for now) a vulgar type II manipulator who thinks only of his interest without worrying about mine?"

The answer is sometimes cruel, and it often takes courage to accept the evidence.

Ask yourself the following question: "The last time I gave in to this kind of manipulation, was the manipulator worth the price of my sacrifice?"

The Manipulator Uses Preconceptions

The Situation

Preconceived ideas are what everyone thinks about a situation. They are what is accepted by society and that no one would think to question (one must be honest, one should not lie, one must be generous). All of these convictions represent an essential pillar of our education, without which life in society would not be possible.

The manipulator plays on these beliefs (which always contain some truth) and diverts them to his advantage if we deny him what he asks, he will try to make us feel guilty by saying, "Those who do not know how to share are selfish!"

A kind grandmother created serious conflicts by saying with great conviction: "In the family we can say everything." The one who was opposed to her was interrupted by this other idea: "You must respect my white hair."

According to their needs and circumstances, the manipulator will use one or another of these ready-made ideas to enslave us better. He can state a certain number of ready-made sentences: "It is not easy to refuse when you ask politely... We must always help others... We must trust... We must know how to be helpful... We must not leave people in need..."

He may also attempt to impose his will in holding forth: "You can never go wrong if... Always keep your word... It is easier to escape problems than to solve them..."

For the manipulator, ready-made ideas are an extraordinary means of pressure because they impose on us as universal truths that it would be out of place to question. These are true conditioned reflexes that nobody doubts. And yet, this is what should be done because no ready-made idea can prove to be accurate at all times and under all circumstances.

Remember

Thus, the expression "he who does not attempt anything has nothing" can encourage someone who is hesitant to become self-employed or can manipulate someone who is hesitant to take drugs or to do any other stupid activity.

To Resist

When a manipulator uses a ready-made idea, one must not remain a prisoner of what he assures us with confidence. You have to use common sense and question him (or ask yourself) by asking, "So what?" Then, depending on the answer obtained, the question must be repeated: "So what?" We continue like this until we escape manipulation.

"You should help me, I am your friend. (First idea ready.) And then?"

"With friends, it is normal to help each other. (the Second idea ready.)"

"So what?"

"I need 1,000 €."

"I'm sorry, but I do not have that much money to lend."

"What about 500 €, could you?"

"Look, right now, I can not lend money to anyone, and it has nothing to do with friendship. Okay?"

"Okay."

To overcome personal blockages that temporarily prevent us from resisting or opposing the manipulator, we can use the exercise by questioning ourselves.

Someone previously convinced you to help them, and now you cannot do it anymore.

"I promised to help him."

"So what?"

"When one commits oneself, one must always keep one's word."

"And then?"

"Now I can't really help them anymore."

"So what?"

"He will not be happy."

"So what?"

"After all, it's his problem and he did not give me a choice."

"So what?"

"I'll call him to explain the situation."

It is not the manipulator who makes us dependent, it is the

ready-made ideas that we accept without questioning them. By questioning these ready-made ideas, the technique of "So what?!" can resist or defuse a large number of type II manipulations.

Chapter 7 - Why Can't You Say No?

We all already know how to say no. In situations where we are comfortable, and when we dominate the situation, we are not afraid to assert ourselves by clearly showing our refusal. For example, it is not difficult to say no to a small child or to an adult that we do not fear.

We also know how to say no in response to an inappropriate gesture or a completely unacceptable proposal. In this case, it is the legitimacy of our anger that gives us sufficient strength to dare to say no.

But between these two extremes, there are many situations where it is difficult to oppose someone. For example, it is not easy to say no to a boss who asks for extra work, to a colleague who embarrasses us, to a friend who invites himself at the wrong time or to a salesman who is too persuasive.

The problem is not knowing how to say no, it is that we need to dare to tell the right person at the right time. But to oppose and manifest a refusal, one must not be in submission. To assert oneself serenely in the face of a manipulator, one must be able to claim one's right to exist as a free person. This is called assertiveness.

Those who have received a lot of love in their childhood, those who received many congratulations and who have been encouraged in their initiatives are less sensitive to manipulation because they have great confidence in themselves. On the other hand, those who have received more criticism than praise naturally show a serious lack of trust and are easy prey for manipulators.

The origins of this lack of self-confidence are numerous. However, we can classify them under three headings:

- The Fear of Authority

- Guilt

- The Need to Be Loved (or the Fear of Being Rejected)

The Fear of Authority

The fear of authority is the paralyzed child facing his father, who scolds him. It is also what subjects us to the authority of a professor, a chief, a judge, a police officer, a doctor, or any other "respectable" figure. Through our education, we have been taught to respect and especially not to contradict the authority.

The reflex of submission hampers self-assertion. And people who do not dare to assert themselves are the ones who respond primarily to the needs of others before thinking of their own. It is understandable that, under these conditions, it is rather difficult to oppose and dare to say no.

The fear of being judged selfish (or even, wicked, ungrateful, or a bad parent) or the fear of conflict are two other forms of fear of authority. Becoming aware of this, often unconscious, the reflex is a salutary first step to start trusting one's own judgment instead of submitting oneself unconditionally to others. We can ask for advice and recommendations without being forced to follow them to the letter as if they were orders of divine right.

In order to no longer depend on the judgment of others and to be able to assert your own point of view, answer quietly each of these three questions: Who has the most knowledge and information about me? Who is best placed to know me and judge me? Can anyone know me better than I know myself? Return to the first question and repeat this exercise several times until you begin to feel good (the feeling of your own conviction). At this point, ask yourself: As a last resort, who is best placed to decide what to do, say, or think?

The Feeling of Guilt

Whether the guilt has a real cause (or invented) or whether it has been suggested or imposed by a manipulator, in either case, this feeling asserts itself without any assistance.

Developing a sense of guilt has many consequences and is counterbalancing, among other things, assertiveness. Thus, we sometimes tend to punish ourselves by restricting or weakening our power so as not to start acting badly again. In other cases, the feeling of guilt requires us to let ourselves be led by others (in order to avoid making a mistake). Finally, we can fight each other by imposing constraints of all kinds and by preventing ourselves from succeeding to avoid harming, destroying, or misusing our power.

In any case and for whatever reason, guilt only hinders the freedom to be and the assertion of oneself. One can always repair a fault actually committed, but it is useless to feel guilty without undertaking anything positive. As for the imaginary culpabilities, only in-depth work done with outside help will clarify the situation.

Take all the time you need and make a list of all that you can blame yourself for and who makes you feel guilty. Then, calmly try to determine how each of these memories undermines your self-confidence and hampers the success of your projects.

The recognition and acceptance of the facts free the feeling of guilt associated with it. Generally, it provides a pleasant feeling of power restored.

The Need to Be Loved and the Fear of Being Rejected

This double need hampers the ability to decide and to impose. It can result in questions like:

- Did I do a good job?

- Does she appreciate what I told her?

- Will he appreciate what I bring him?

- What does she think about me?

The opinion of others about what we say or what we do is essential to living and work in groups. It is a form of feedback that allows us to know if what we are doing is what the other person is waiting for. But some are far too attentive to the judgment others will bear on them and think (wrongly) that the opinion of others is a valid evaluation of their own person. We can not live, like a badly licked bear, by ignoring our surroundings and listening to the judgment of others too much. If we identify ourselves too much with what they think of us, we run the risk of existing only through their eyes and according to their opinion.

The mechanism at work is then the following:

- The more I pay attention to what others say about me, the less I trust my own judgment.

- The less I trust myself, the more I need to be reassured about my own worth, and the more I need to feel loved and appreciated by others. The more I try to please others (so that they love me and do not reject me), the more I am attentive to their judgment and the more dependent I am.

We are confronted with an infernal spiral which, with each cycle, transforms us a little more into a puppet that others shape to their measure and whose strings they pull. In these conditions, it is difficult to love oneself, difficult to allow oneself to exist, and even more difficult to say no.

To quench this thirst for love and soothe the fear of being rejected, we will do everything to give ourselves a good image. We try to please others and to avoid making waves. We make sure to match the expectations of others. We are ready to sacrifice ourselves, to always render service to others, to refuse nothing, to avoid conflicts... In a word, we are ready to let ourselves be manipulated.

The solution is simple. Just remember that we (and not others) have the most information about ourselves. We are therefore best placed to have an idea of what we want. Once again, we can listen to outside advice (useful sources of information), but no one is obliged to follow them, let alone believe them. It's up to us to decide what we are worth and what we want.

- An exercise you can try, although it is a little surprising, can be very useful to help you get rid of the weight of the opinion of others about you. Think about a dish, vegetable, or drink you really do not like.

Example: Noodles with water.

Ask yourself the following question: How would this food react if it learned that I do not like it?

Some possible answers: That would leave it feeling cold; it would not affect it; it would not care very much.

Now find a situation where you had the feeling of being rejected.

Answer: Think back to this same situation by adopting the same attitude as the food when it learns that you do not like it.

(I observe this event with the same point of view as a dish of water noodles learning that I do not like it...)

Repeat the exercise (from the beginning and with the help of others examples) until you reach a state of detachment that is sufficient compared to the negative judgment of others.

- A second exercise can be performed, following a similar method. Find a situation in which you did not know how to or could not oppose someone.

Determine what type of fear was causing your inability to react (fear of authority, feeling guilty, fear of not being loved anymore).

Check if your fear is still justified today.

Repeat the exercise as many times as you wish until you reach satisfactory conclusions.

Chapter 8 - How to Say No

Why are people so mean? Why are they so selfish? Why can some people not be trusted? Why?

Most people who find it hard to say no have one thing in common: they find the world hostile, and they would like to be able to live quietly without being continually forced to be on the defensive.

It is regrettable that the world is filled with crooks, egotists, and manipulators of all kinds. We can regret that we can no longer trust anyone, but these recriminations do not change the case. There is no point in playing the ostrich while regretting that the world is bad or difficult. To moan about the harshness of life (or to dream of a better world) prevents one from seeing reality and, therefore, from acting effectively. As we dream of an impossible world, the one we live in becomes hostile, and we feel less and less able to change anything.

To dare to say no, one must first accept to see the world as it is. There are selfish people, others who are thirsty for power, there are manipulators, there are also cheaters, liars... There will be a long list. It is useless to groan or lament, this is how the world is made. Let's open our eyes and accept the facts!

How to Say No to a Charming Manipulator

The Finding

Whether a man a woman or a child, the charming manipulator draws us and lulls us in an illusion because we found the manipulator attractive, fun, touching, friendly, etc. He seems so full of attractions that we would like, in return, if not please him at least not to displease him.

His art of seduction paralyzes us and prevents us from saying no to him. We are afraid of disappointing him, we are afraid of appearing ridiculous, we do not want to be seen as "stingy", jaded or selfish. As long as we believe in the image presented to us by the charming manipulator, we do not dare to resist him, and so we find it difficult to say no to him.

To Resist

Facing a charming manipulator, the first thing to do is to break through the illusions. To achieve this, one can ask oneself the following questions: what do these smiles and beautiful manners hide, what is his real purpose, and what does he really want from me? Beyond what he shows me where does his interest lie? Why is he doing all this? In this story, who will be the real winner? Where is the trap?

Then, to put an end to small manipulations, the simplest is still to say no with the firm intention not to go further in the discussion. This no must be clear, clean, unscrupulous and must not engender any sense of guilt. Do not be afraid to oppose the manipulator! There is really no danger in saying no to a charming manipulator who asks you for a service or tries to sell you something.

Remember that you cannot hurt a manipulator. We can only hurt honest people. If a manipulator told you that you hurt him, do not believe him and especially do not enter his game. It is still an attempt to manipulate to make you give way to his request.

The real goal of the manipulative charmer is not to please you, but to take advantage of your credulity, one way or another. Also, do not give him time to develop his arguments and convince you. Time (the length of discussion) always plays in his favor. Each additional second spent listening to it makes you fall a little deeper into his trap.

Remember that you are in the presence of a Type II manipulator who thinks only of his interests (even if he says he only thinks of yours). Abbreviate! Tell him no, simply and as quickly as possible.

To say no is both to affirm one's refusal and one's willingness to put an end to communication. By saying, no thank you, or no it does not interest me, the intention must be clear, concise, and straightforward. No ulterior motives or scruples! Above all, no guilt! The more perceptible your confidence and assertiveness, the more effective your refusal, and the more the manipulator's maneuvers will be quickly stopped.

Sometimes we cannot just say no in a simple way. Either we waited too long, or we know the person too well. In these circumstances, it is better to know how to formulate your refusal correctly.

When we do not want or when we cannot meet the expectations of a charming manipulator, we must know how to say no in these forms.

A friend asks you to take her somewhere when you have to go to an appointment: "It would be really nice of you if you could drive me to a place."

Rather than giving in and missing your appointment, you tell her no, as follows:

"Look, I gladly would have accompanied you, but it is at the other end of town, and I have this appointment that I absolutely cannot push back. Maybe you could take a taxi or ask someone else to take you? Now forgive me, but I must go."

Let's take a closer look at this kind of answer as it contains all the necessary ingredients to say no to a charming manipulator.

You first show him that you understood his request and that

you are not against it, but you absolutely cannot do her this service: "Look, I would have gladly accompanied you, but it is up to the other end of the city, and I have this appointment that I absolutely cannot push back. . ."

You then offer her an alternative without giving her time to breathe. "You could maybe take a taxi or ask someone else to take you."

Finally, on your way, you cleanly break from the interaction under a valid excuse, and you leave the scene: "Now forgive me, but I must go."

To say no in this manner:

- Describe the situation by repeating the words of the manipulator to show unambiguously that you understand the nature of the request.

- Calmly express your point of view or expose your constraints without justifying or losing yourself in useless details: I cannot or I do not want to do it for this or that reason.

- Search for and propose one or more solutions: Maybe you could... Have you thought to ask...

- Put an end to the conversation with a short sentence to signify to the person you are talking to, that for you, the communication is over: Well, I hope you will find a solution. Good luck and goodbye!

"Do you want to buy into the lottery with me? It will cost us less, and we will share the winnings."

"Thank you for thinking about me, but you know I do not like gambling. If you win, I prefer that you keep everything. I do not say "good luck" since it seems that it brings bad luck."

The sense of repartee or appropriateness is not invented. It is a form of ease that is born with an understanding of things and grows with self-confidence.

A person who is sure of herself is not afraid to express her point of view firmly and calmly. She defends her rights while respecting those of others. She is able to assert her personality and needs without provoking hostility. She does not let herself be walked on and knows how to say no without feeling guilty.

Remember

To overcome a charming manipulator, you must first realize that behind the charmer hides a manipulator. Discovering one's hidden purpose is one of the best ways to break the spell. In order to put an end to the simplest manipulation is to dare to assert your refusal quietly and without excess complexity. Depending on the context and the quality of the relationship, the expression of no will be more or less realized in the ways we discussed above.

How to Say No to a Guilty Manipulator

As far as most type II manipulations are concerned, you have to know how to say no to get rid of them. Unfortunately, some manipulators still manage to extort what they want by playing on our feelings of guilt. In this case, saying no is not enough.

The Observation

Here is a non-exhaustive series of guilt phrases used by a manipulator:

- Listen, I am your friend, you cannot refuse me that!

- After all, I've done for you, is how you reward me?

- I never denied you anything, and you had the nerve to say no to me...

- You only think about yourself, and I had cared about you completely!

- How dare you do such a thing?

- It's always the same thing, as soon as I ask for something, I'm refused ...thing

The essential thing is to understand that the guilt-maker tries to play with our conscience and make us feel bad. In this way, he strives to make us regret our refusal and thus intends to change our minds. See how some beggars know how to play in this register to get the passer-by to open his wallet more easily.

Find one or two situations in which the manipulator was able to make you feel guilty when he countered your refusal, or simply to better get you to give him what he wanted.

Guilt is an honorable feeling that is related to our education. Our parents, school, friends, and life in society taught us what was good and what was not. In the same way, we learned, often at our expense, what it cost to break an established code.

Guilt is also a natural feeling in the normal man. Only the great perverts, war criminals, terrorists, serial killers, pedophiles, and other sick people feel absolutely no remorse. When they are called to trial, they are completely insensitive to the evocation of their crimes. It is this indifference and lack of compassion that disturbs the victims and their families (as they testify in front of the cameras at the end of the courtroom).

Guilt is a normal and easily accessible emotion. The skill of the guilty manipulator is to know how to activate it wrongly in his victim. It is not the guilt itself that is in question, but its justification. As long as we do not carefully study this feeling to question it, eventually, the manipulator manages to make us submit. In fact, he wins as long as we believe we should be guilty.

To Resist

To resist a guilty manipulator the question to ask is: Am I really guilty of what I am accused of? The answer is not easy, and it is not a question of disguising yourself as a justice of the peace to determine who is wrong and who is right. What counts is to know how to evaluate, even approximately, the reality of guilt. For that, it is enough to ask: Is there a balance between what he asks me and what he says he gave me?

A friend requires you to come and help him move, and you absolutely cannot do it:

"Say, I'm counting on you to help me move next Thursday."

"You know I cannot, I'm already taken."

"I thank you! When you needed me, you were happy to find me. Now that I need you, you drop me like an old sock."

You actually remember that you had invited this friend to help you restore your country house. In fact, he got up at 11 o'clock and did not participate in any work, even housework. From time to time, he came to see if we needed him and went back to take a nap or go for a walk. Now, thanks to this quick review, you can answer him calmly. "Yes, I was very happy to have friends to help me when I needed it. It was a good holiday for everyone. Besides, you have benefited well. But when it comes to your move, I really cannot help you, I'm already taken elsewhere. Ask someone else or call a company."

When we find ourselves in the presence of a guilty manipulator, and we realize that there was no reason to feel guilty, we can then oppose him calmly and tell him no without needing to justify.

In spite of what he tells you, you owe him nothing. Do not embark on endless explanations either. Abbreviate the conversation without complexity, avoiding aggression, devaluation, and irony.

Guilt and Legitimacy

The desire and the will of others are legitimate, but that is not a reason for them to impose their will on us by making us feel guilty. We also have needs and aspirations just as legitimate. To regain our legitimacy, in the face of this feeling of guilt, it is essential to take a little time to reflect on our present and future rights.

To help you feel confident when faced with guilt, study and complete the list below.

I have the right: to think differently from you; to rest; to do what I want; to not make myself do it; to not always agree; to work at my pace; to think about me; not to love; to refuse; not to give any explanation...

The Right to the Difference

To widen this reflection on the legitimacy of your rights, remember situations where someone has prevented you from asserting your own taste or expressing your preferences, your opinions, your feelings, and your reactions.

Take the time to see how you could have asserted yourself more with what you know now. Do it for each of your rights. This is not lost time, quite the opposite!

The Right to Imperfection

Know that you are not a superman or a wonder woman. You have the right to have weaknesses and to display your limits and your misunderstandings. There is no objective reason to be guilty of these "inadequacies".

These are not flaws but are simply proof of our humanity. In this case too, see how you could have reacted differently by claiming these rights without making it complicated instead of hiding them.

Remember

The guilt or the threat of rejection are ways that the guilty manipulator uses to enslave us. By becoming aware of our stagnation (which submits us to blackmail), we free ourselves from both guilt and manipulation. We are then able to assert ourselves for what we are and become able to say no to manipulation.

How to Say No to a Respectable Manipulator

The difficulty with respectable manipulators is that one does not even think of telling them no simply because one does not realize that one is being manipulated.

The Observation

When a doctor, a journalist or someone with a higher social status than ours speaks, we tend to listen to him and believe him without question. Respectability fascinates. It is enough for information to be signed by a researcher or announced by a known journalist to become credible. If it's written in the newspaper or seen on TV, it's a seal of validity that makes us accept the message without further ado.

In 1986, when we were told that the radioactive cloud of Chernobyl had stopped at the borders of France, few people thought to question the words of the ministers and those of the journalists who reported the case. It took years for public opinion to become aware of the manipulation and its consequences. In the same way, the tainted blood scandal was based on the respectability of those who knew but manipulated the public by saying the opposite.

Around us, there are many respectable people who are worthy of being respected, but there are also those who disappoint us or who betray us. Regarding the latter, we only realize it when it is too late. Indeed, hypnotized by the knowledge, fame, social status, or ascendancy of someone, one does not think to put his word in doubt.

Manipulation through respectability is, for example, a friend who was thought to be loyal but who repeats what she was told to keep quiet. It is the partner, the banker, or the notary (professions oh so respectable), in whom one had placed all his confidence, and that ruin us by starting suddenly with the cashier. It is the husband who cheats on his wife when she believes him to be faithful, the politician who lies to us to be reelected, or the honorable journalist who distorts or "falsifies" the information to be the first to share a story.

When we experience manipulation done by someone respectable, we feel a deep sense of injustice related to the feeling of betrayal. The disappointment is commensurate with the trust or respect one had for that person. Whose fault is it? Does it always affect the person who is accused of having betrayed us, or are we partly responsible for being too naive? The problem posed by the maneuvers of a respectable manipulator is complex because the responsibility is shared between the manipulator and the manipulated. Although it may seem strange (at first glance), a tale of ANDERSEN, "The Emperor's Clothes", will allow us to bring to light this subtle mechanism.

Illustration

Once upon a time, a long time ago, in a country very different from ours, an emperor was passionate about new clothes. In order to please his people, he changed his costume at every opportunity and had one for each hour of each day of the year.

One day, two crooks who called themselves weavers, came to see him and told him that they were able to make the most beautiful fabric. Not only would the colors and designs be exceptional, but this fabric would also have the incredible property of being invisible to incompetents and fools.

Subjugated by the words of these eminent specialists, the Emperor exclaimed: "What a marvel! I want and I demand that you wear a suit made from this stuff. I will be able to discover who serves me competently and distinguish intelligent people from imbeciles.

It will be much easier for me to govern because I will know how to behave."

To close the deal, he agreed to a significant advance and helped them set up by exempting them from taxes. The two accomplices established their looms in a chic neighborhood of the city and obtained large quantities of bristles (the finest), gold and silver threads, and countless precious stones, as many treasures as they could. To give credence to the illusion, they pretended to work on their machines which were actually running empty and stayed late at night in their workshop closed to the public.

Sometime later, the excited and impatient emperor wanted to know where the work was. He, therefore, sent his best minister, whom he trusted, to report to him on the work of the weavers. When he arrived there, the minister was very surprised to find that the two weavers were working on empty crafts. His experience in diplomacy made it clear that he should not give himself away, and although he was troubled, he made no comment.

As he approached, the two weavers described to him their work: "Is not it wonderful, look at these colors, admire these lovely designs that we created especially for the emperor. What do you say, is not it absolutely sumptuous?"

The poor minister's eyes widened as he saw nothing that the two crooks described with passion. He thought, "Shall I be a fool or an incompetent? It is unthinkable! No one must know, much less suspect, that I do not see this stuff." He answered aloud, "Oh! It is absolutely delightful, these colors, I do not know how to express my admiration. I will speak of them to the

Emperor, who will be absolutely delighted. You can believe me because I am his most faithful servant."

"That encourages us," said the two weavers, smiling. Then they handed to the Emperor's minister an elegant confidential file to fill in his information, and the clerk went to the door with all the deference due to his rank.

Concerned about the situation, and before going to see the Emperor, the Minister nevertheless took the precaution of sending one of his advisers to make a second visit to the two weavers.

The latter went to visit the workshop and carefully inspected the looms on which the crooks wove, very diligently, and of course, always without the slightest touch. "Is this stuff not beautiful?" They asked, showing him and explaining to him their invisible work. "Your minister admired it a great deal during his last visit."

"I am however, not a fool" said the adviser before continuing, "my diplomas prove that I am not incompetent. All this is very strange, but I must leave nothing to it." He then praised what he did not see and warmly congratulated them on their work. Returning to the ministry, he prepared his report by skillfully using the arguments and words that the two weavers had used to convince him.

Comforted by this testimony, the minister then went to the

Emperor to tell him all the good he thought about the work of the two weavers. On leaving the Emperor's office, the minister was interviewed by a large number of journalists. The rumor about the beauty of the stuff was huge, and everybody was talking about it. One said he knew about the origin of the drawings, another knew someone from Europe who had seen the fabric. People even placed bets to see when the clothes would be finished.

At last, the big moment arrived. The two crooks, who had been working all night to put the finishing touches on their work, entered the great audience hall of the Emperor. In the presence of all the dignitaries, they undressed the Emperor and then pretended to give him his new clothes. They exclaimed: "Feel how light these clothes are, so much that you will think you do not have them on your body. Your majesty is of an unheard-of elegance. We've never seen anything like it!"

While the emperor was tossing and turning in front of the large mirror, admiring courtiers commented about the beauty of the costume loudly, "God, you're beautiful, as these colors go together so well! We have never seen such a beautiful suit, as well worn. These drawings are splendid! It is both classic and revolutionary. Believe me, it's really art, we'll continue to talk about it for a long time, and it's an expert who tells you that."

Nobody had the words to proclaim their admiration. There were even some women who faked a faint before the king. Each one, anxious to prove that he was neither stupid nor incompetent, endeavored to show that he saw the clothes.

The enthusiasm was such that the emperor decided to show this splendor to the people immediately. The announcement was made, and the parade was organized in the blink of an eye. The two crooks approached the monarch and carefully hooked on a huge trail of the same fabric, and then humbly recoiled under the applause and cheers of the audience. Nobody wanted to show that he saw nothing, the procession moved and went through the city. A large crowd came to admire the event. Everyone applauded. Here and there we heard a few laughs, but they were quickly covered by a "hush!"

However, a little child's voice came through the crowd: "He is naked, gentleman. Why does he not wear a coat?" His father, who carried him on his shoulders, exclaimed "Listen to the voice of innocence. Listen to what this child says to you!"

Hearing these words, the emperor realized what was happening, but he did nothing to show his realization. Enough about the small wind that swept the city, he said to himself: "This child must be right, but I must keep up the show until the end of the procession." The imperial cortege thus continued its course, and the ministers continued to carry a trail that did not exist while some fanatics sang: "The Emperor is naked, the Emperor is naked."

Fortunately, the police watched, and everything quickly

returned to normal. The costume was placed in a safe as a national treasure, and the two weavers were awarded the highest honors from the country. Later, their name was even given to an imperial weaving school.

Let's draw together the teachings of this tale.

Exercise

Take a few moments to try to determine the real culprits of this manipulation. Are they the weavers or one of the victims of the manipulation?

First Lesson

The first lesson to be learned from this story is that the one who needs recognition is placed under the authority of the person whom he wishes to draw attention to. The emperor seeks the admiration of his subjects to keep his power as long as possible. Ministers and courtiers copy the emperor to be noticed and to obtain the best positions in the government. Finally, the subjects themselves want to show that they are not inferior to the great ones of this world by behaving like them.

The thirst for recognition and the need for identification create a dependency that opens the door to manipulation. Thus, adolescents who want to exist on their own are, at the same time very sensitive to the behavior of their idols. They copy their ways of dressing, styling, or behaving. This mimicry is a way for them to appear different from adults and to oppose what they know of the world they are discovering. But if this challenge to the established order can be a source of renewal, it also places these young people under the manipulative dependence of opinion makers, gurus, sects, and other unscrupulous people who know how to exploit their enthusiasm and their nobility.

Later, when teenagers have become adults, they still do the same thing. For the sake of compliance or fear of being rejected by their community, they continue to duplicate the most characteristic behaviors. They obey the "politically correct" of their generation, their social category, or their professional environment. To be accepted and recognized by those whom they consider respectable, they speak, think, and consume as they do. They follow their advice and submit to their laws. But for lack of hindsight, they quickly become slaves to the taste of others and are, one might say, "manipulated without the knowledge of their own free will".

To avoid being and acting like the emperor's courtiers, one of these questions may arise: Who should I please, and what is my opinion? Why do I want to think like others? Am I me? What would happen if I did not think like the others? Why do I want to be admired? What will happen if they reject me? Are there other possible points of view?

After re-reading the tale, try to imagine how each manipulated person might not have fallen into the trap of the weavers by asking one or the other of the questions above.

Second Lesson

The second lesson of the tale was that respectability is in the imagination of the one who bows to the people he thinks, rightly or wrongly, to be estimable. Respect must not be demanded, it must be deserved.

The real question is: How can you recognize someone really respectable? Really respectable people are easy and enjoyable. They make you feel smart, and you can easily understand what they are saying. Listening to them makes you feel bigger, smarter, and more confident. Someone truly respectable listens to what is said to him. He seeks to help those who approach him grow, and if he believes that someone is superior to him, he seeks to understand and feed on his knowledge.

Conversely, the respectable manipulator degrades those who surpass him and pushes those who are inferior to him. For fear of ridicule, we dare not question his word. If you do, he is surprised at your ignorance. For him, it is always very simple and obvious, but his explanations explain nothing. He gives references without worrying about whether others understand or know what they are about.

Whether he is a politician, a journalist, a doctor, a lawyer, or a guru, he must first appear eminently respectable before he can be taken seriously. He, therefore, relies on his appearance to impress or defraud his victims and uses others to enhance himself.

The respectable manipulator is also based on the idea that we should not doubt people whose job is to know about something. It works with people who are afraid to appear uneducated, rough, or ignorant. Fashion and snobbery are also based on fear of not being like others or of culturally or politically incorrect behavior.

Take a break and find several situations in which a manipulator has manipulated you by using so-called respectability. Then answer the following question: What impressed you the most about him?

Third Lesson

The third lesson to be learned from this tale is that in front of any situation where others are manipulated, one can take the perspective of a child. But having a child's perspective does not mean being absolutely different from others. It is also not a question of ignoring or rejecting divergent ideas and opinions.

To have a child's perspective is first and foremost not to be conditioned. It is to be able to hear and to take into account what others are saying without being dependent on and blindly following them. It is to know how to relate to what they say in order to form a personal opinion. It is free in judgment, regardless of what others may think, however respectable they may be.

You have to know how to cultivate doubt. To take a step back and avoid being manipulated, here are the kinds of questions to ask yourself: What is the interest of this person? What does he really think? What is he trying to make me believe? What does he want me to think? How is this respectable? Can we imagine anything else? Is there another way of seeing things? Is it true? How can I check it? Where can I find other sources of information, other points of view?

Ask yourself any of these questions after reading an article, listening to the radio, or watching the news.

By coming out of our familiar patterns of thinking and acting, often connected to the desire to do what others do, one becomes able to see things and people as they are and not as we imagine them or as they define themselves.

To avoid being trapped by the respectability of notables, the media, those with power, those who know, sects, sellers of good ideas, extremists, and other donors of ready-made solutions, it is necessary to have a fresh look, able to ignore these illusions and to perceive the reality that is hidden behind appearances.

Remember

We are often trapped because of the respect that we give (instinctively) to those who know. The problem is not so much knowing or daring to say no to respectable manipulators, it is above all necessary to know how to recognize them in order to avoid being trapped. Whoever finds his child's gaze is no longer impressed by the judgment or the approval of others, and he is able to say, "The king is naked."

How to Say No to an Authoritarian Manipulator

The authoritarian manipulator uses force or violence to obtain what he wants. Not feeling that he is powerful enough, he intimidates or seeks to belittle others so that he can better impose his will. That's why we're afraid to say no to him.

The authoritarian manipulator is a weak and often cowardly person who controls his victims as long as they fear him. The solution is not in submission and even less in flight. It is necessary to understand better how an authoritarian manipulator works so as not to be impressed by the artifices he uses to put us in a state of inferiority.

Why Do We Submit to Authority?

Starting at a young age, we are taught to submit to the rules of life in society. When the young child refuses to obey, his parents raise their voices. They tell him that he is not nice that he should feel sorry for them or that they do not like him anymore. When that is not enough, they take sanctions. The result is that the child quickly discovers the dangers of disobedience and likens them to possible rejection. He repeats to himself incessantly: "If I do not do what my parents ask me, they will not love me anymore." He understands quickly that by obeying he will please his parents and that by disobeying he will be reprimanded (which for him is synonymous with rejection).

To be loved, the child, therefore, accepts the prohibitions imposed upon him until he transgresses them and thus feels guilty of treason against those who have laid down these taboos. But he also discovers that to obey means to please the other, to disobey is also to satisfy his personal wishes and desires: "I want to eat jam because it would make me happy. But I know that I risk being scolded because it's forbidden."

Thus, over time, he feels increasingly guilty of giving free rein to his desires and having fun. When disobedience generates (almost systematically) a deep sense of guilt, it becomes very difficult to disobey, oppose, say no to someone, or break a rule.

At home, then at school, the will or desires of others are

imposed on him and restrict his freedom. By unconsciously accepting the prohibitions and submitting to the authority of others, it is increasingly difficult for him to indulge himself, to dare to assert himself and to oppose the abusive authority.

The mechanism of obedience works because you want to be loved, because you refuse to be rejected, or because you do not want to feel guilty.

To Resist

Authoritarian manipulation works as long as one lets oneself go and is afraid to react. From the moment we understand what elements this manipulation is based on, it becomes possible to do something and act effectively.

If you experience authoritarian manipulation, start by looking for the nature of the mechanism in question. This is either a need for recognition or the fear of feeling guilty.

Need for Recognition

If you cannot defend yourself from authoritarian manipulation, take a few moments to look for what is paralyzing you. Do you obey because you need to be recognized, loved, or appreciated by the manipulator or do you fear that he will reject you if you do not do what he asks you? When you have isolated the desire or fear that compels you to submit, observe whether the esteem, friendship, or love of that person deserves all this trouble.

To help you make this assessment, make a list of the advantages and disadvantages of letting yourself go. This search is complete as soon as you feel free to take action.

Guilt

If you do not feel empowered to defend yourself or feel guilty about disobeying, take the time to think about the value of guilt. Look for the unconscious message that tells you not to react, it may be something innocuous: "We do not respond that way to adults... We must obey our boss... A woman must follow her husband... He is more knowledgeable than me... If he says it is true, he must be correct since he is the authority... You must always follow the rules... I must not be selfish... We must sacrifice ourselves for others..."

When have you found one or more injunctions ask yourself: "Why do I think that? What is the proof that it is true? Why should I continue to believe it?"

Continue this investigative work until you feel released from this so-called guilt.

Let's leave the past in its place! We are often more intimidated by the memory of authoritarian people than by the interlocutor present in front of us. In this kind of situation, we do not dare to defend ourselves because the manipulator reminds us of someone who made a big difference when we were young and impressionable. For example, it may be the memory of a very demanding parent, a hard-working authoritarian teacher, or anyone else who intimidated or terrorized us as children.

Find out who this authoritarian manipulator makes you think of, then note the similarities between the manipulator of today and that of yesterday. To finish, specify their differences.

This research is interesting because by knowing how to tell the difference between the past and the present, one frees himself from the weight of his memories and one no longer fights against shadows. By clearly realizing the present situation and perceiving the manipulator as they are (in the present moment), one is less and less a victim of his habits and more and more capable of reacting correctly.

Let's get past the fear of conflict! To oppose an authority figure whether they are manipulative or not is to feel guilty of disobeying and it is also running the risk of annoying or irritating the other. By fearing conflict, one merely places an additional asset in the hands of the authoritarian manipulator.

To overcome this fear of conflict or to learn not to be afraid to disobey, let's start by correctly assessing the risks.

What do I really risk? After clearly observing an authoritarian manipulation, answer these questions (we have provided a non-exhaustive list):

- What will happen to me if I really oppose an authoritarian character?

- What will happen if I do not obey?

- At worst, what can happen to me?

- If the worst should happen, how can I avoid it or limit the damage?

- Can I really be sure of what will happen?

- How is this situation different from all the others?

- If this has happened in the past, should it necessarily happen again this time?

If authoritarian manipulation works, it is because the victims cannot or do not dare to defend themselves. As long as they cannot assert themselves and accept being dominated, they will be controlled by the manipulator.

We must start by respecting ourselves so that others respect us too. To reclaim the legitimate right to think and to say no is to allow oneself to assert oneself, to exist, to be.

Let's find our own legitimacy! After identifying an authoritarian manipulator, ask yourself the following questions (another non-exhaustive list).

- Why am I forced to believe him without thinking?

- In this case, am I really obliged to obey him?

- How can I do otherwise?

- Why do I tremble in front of him?

- Why am I obliged to do what he tells me?

- How can I see things differently?

- How is he really superior to me?

- Is it reasonable to fear him to the point of saying nothing?

- Am I allowed to have a different viewpoint?

- How is my point of view less respectable than his?

- That's what he says, but is he really right?

- What attitude should be adopted?

Remember

Opposing authoritarian manipulation is, to a certain extent, being able to say no to the old reflexes of the past (especially those of one's childhood and education). But it is also to overcome the fear of conflict and to look at the world with a child's eyes. Before being able to say no to an authoritarian manipulator, one must find enough legitimacy to give oneself the right to exist, to think for oneself, and to express one's own point of view.

Chapter 9 - Tools to Say No

With this chapter, we present a certain number of tools to help the reader better face various manipulations. These are useful weapons and will be especially useful for those who understood the mechanisms of manipulation and who also overcame the mental blocks and fears which prevented them from opposing manipulation.

Whatever the type of manipulation encountered, to say no to a manipulator, there are a number of principles to respect, when and in the order that suits you best.

The Tools of Analysis

First of all, you have to start by understanding what is going on. For that, we ask ourselves a certain number of questions: What is it? What is happening? What's the problem?

The situation is well framed when one is able to answer these questions clearly and adopt a precise formulation: He wants me to give him... He is trying to... He would like...

To think in this way avoids getting lost on the wrong track and getting lost in problems that do not exist or that do not concern us. Many people frustrate themselves with useless sentences by appropriating the problems of others or by trying to provide answers that people do not require.

Find a situation in which you helped someone who had not asked you for anything and see how it turned against you.

Identify the Type of Manipulation

This work is an important step to avoid the trap of manipulation or to get out of it. Indeed, taking the time to ask if we are in the presence of a manipulator whether a charmer, one who guilts us or is respectable or authoritarian, one takes a step back from the situation, one acquires more insurance and we let ourselves become less susceptible.

After discovering that it is a charming manipulator, we are more on guard because we know it is difficult to refuse what he asks. This awareness prevents us from falling into the trap he gives us or prepares us to get out of it. After identifying a guilty manipulator, we will think to weigh what he said he gave us with what he asks us. We will also be less upset by his attacks and will better defend ourselves.

By unmasking a respectable manipulator who puts on a dazzling show in our presence, we see it from another eye, and we listen differently. If we give up the blasphemy, we will find a child's eyes to guess his intentions better and thwart his maneuvers.

Finally, understanding that we are facing an authoritarian manipulator, we become less accessible to his maneuvers. We are aware of his attempts to impress us by playing on our old desire to be loved, on our sense of obedience and on the feeling of guilt, we might feel in refusing to obey.

By identifying a manipulator for what he is, one runs less risk of being a victim of his maneuvers, and as a result, one can organize his defenses. It's never too late to make this identification, but the faster we act, the less we get caught.

Make the Point

When you feel manipulated or to clear up any misunderstanding, it is necessary to check regularly if one correctly grasped the nature of the request of the manipulator. For that, it is enough to tell him what one thinks to have understood and to ask him then if that is actually what the request is about.

You have the impression that a friend invites you, without telling you clearly whether it is to help him make repairs. To be sure, you can tell him. "If I understand correctly, you want me to come to your house to take advantage of the campaign, but also to help you do some work." In one way or another, he will be obliged to answer clearly, and you will have your answer about the manipulation.

By taking stock of what is confusing, you are no longer trapped, and you can respond to a request that the manipulator had never made clear. Now, you can express your refusal with legitimacy and no trace of guilt.

A type II manipulator tries to sell you an insurance policy you might say, "If I understand correctly, you propose that I buy this insurance policy that protects me from such and such, while I am already covered by another contract." Embarrassed, he is obliged to answer, "Yes, but, with my contract..." Without giving him time to continue, you can then say to him, "Well, thank you, I see that I understood you well and there is nothing else to add. Goodbye, and thank you!"

Here again, the confidence found thanks to this development makes it possible to put an end to the manipulation and to end the conversation without the feeling of guilt.

After a long conversation that allowed Mathilde to make the point with a charming manipulator (who was also very macho) who offered to marry her, she can say with confidence, "If I understand correctly you want to marry me so that I come and live at home to take care of your cat when you are not there and also to do the housework, the cooking, and the dishes. Do you really think that's what I expect from life?"

Most manipulations are based on poorly formulated demands. By verifying, with the manipulator, that you have understood what he asked you (more or less clearly), you are no longer under his influence, and you regain your confidence and your ability to say no.

Tools of the Refusal

To voice one's disagreement or to express one's point of view is not always an easy thing. Some prefer to avoid problems, even if, in the long run, it devalues them because each new difficulty is, in their eyes, additional proof of their inability to solve problems.

When confronted with a manipulation, others choose to attack the opponent. They close themselves off, their features harden, and they are hostile and threatening. Or on the contrary, they wear an ironic smile, and they display expressions signifying contempt or disapproval. This is actually a way to show that we are not fooled and we do not want to let ourselves be trapped. But at the same time, this attitude indicates that one is fragile and therefore not very sure of oneself.

Aggressive behaviors reveal a latent fear, a desire for revenge, or a degree of frustration. Anything that a skilled manipulator will know how to exploit.

Rather than escape or attack, there is a more effective way of asserting oneself and defending one's rights without provoking hostility. This is called serene affirmation.

The Serene Assertion

This last one implies that one must be authentic and not hide one's feelings, while not allowing oneself to walk over other people. Assert yourself serenely. Doing so is to play your cards on the table; it is to be comfortable and to seek a middle ground while controlling the environment. This technique is particularly adapted to fight type II manipulators when it is believed that the manipulators are receptive to logical discussion and understanding of things.

A Technique Comprising Several Stages

The preparatory phase: First of all, we must start by thinking so we can discover and understand the motivations of the manipulator and the benefit (often hidden) that he seeks to gain from his manipulation. It can also be done very simply and quickly.

The second phase corresponding to the meeting with the manipulator:

- Describe to him the situation that he makes you live in, or his behavior towards you, using terms that are as precise and objective as possible. Especially avoid being accusing or expressing guilt.

- Discuss the material or emotional consequences (stress, fatigue...) of his manipulation with him and the upheavals that this causes in your life. Give him your feelings, concerns, and criticisms. This is about talking about yourself and what's happening to you, not about him.

- Suggest a solution, a realistic modification, or a compromise that could put an end to this inconvenience.

- Interest him by showing him the positive effects that he could draw or that would allow the two of you to find what he is missing.

By telling a smoker "Go out and smoke" there is a risk of creating conflict because his purpose is not just to smoke but to relax while smoking. It is therefore likely that he feels assaulted by our request which amounts, for him, to an unfair demand.

On the other hand, things will be much better if we know how to say to him, "I understand that you want to smoke, but it gives me a headache. Would you be able to smoke outside this room where I have to work?"

The second way takes into account the needs of the one who has been frustrating and leads him to change his attitude more easily by making him discover what he had been putting us through.

By saying to someone, "Stop doing this, you annoy me." Or by saying, "Speak more quietly." you send him a message. We accuse him and make him guilty of what we are living with.

The message kills the conversation because it often feels like being blamed, humiliated, criticized, or rejected. To say to someone who taps his pen on the table, "Stop you're annoying me," communicates both a lack of respect and often leads to retaliation.

On the other hand, if one says to him, "When you make this small noise while tapping the pen on the table, it prevents me from concentrating. Could you stop so that I can do my job?" This sends a message that respects the forms of the serene affirmation described above.

From there, it is a safe bet that the interference stops instantly, saying, "Oh, sorry, excuse me!"

It certainly would not have happened if we had said in an angry voice, "Stop teasing me, don't you see I'm working!" In general, messages like this rarely reach the goal that was hoped for.

When a message is correctly formulated, it is perceived by its recipient as a call for help. It also informed him that his problem had been understood, which, in turn, invited him to pay more attention to our concerns. The message dispels emotional reactions and prepares the ground for change. By reformulating a reproach to make it a wish, the message reflects nonverbal feelings and helps to clarify what was unclear.

Responding Quickly and Well

Another important rule for knowing how to say no to a type II manipulator is to respond quickly and well.

Why Respond Quickly?

The longer we say no to a manipulator, the more he feels strong. By not daring to answer, one gives him the impression of being weak. He can also interpret our silence as hesitation. Then, he will gain even more assurance and develop new arguments to convince better or confuse us. By not responding or responding too slowly, we lose all credibility in the eyes of the manipulator who will continue to play with us.

How Can You Answer Well?

This question is interesting because it's about knowing how to measure the power of our answer. For example, if you respond too violently to an authoritarian manipulator, you risk exciting him further and being crushed by his fury. But conversely, if we answer too weakly, we will not appear credible and our answer will not take into account our opposition. So, how can we find the right measure?

As is often the case, the answer will be given by the very person who poses the problem. Indeed, when undergoing a manipulative attack, the safest is to respond with a power corresponding to 90% of the manipulator's.

If someone shouts, do not shout louder than him because you already know that it does not help much. You can try to talk calmly, it works sometimes, but not with a manipulator who will benefit by showing he is stronger. On the other hand, if you answer in the same tone, with a voice that is strong enough and firm, although slightly lower than his, he will pay attention. He will say to himself, "Here is someone who does not let himself be outdone. It would be better for me to be suspicious of him."

By responding quickly and well, with confidence and assurance, you show him that you feel strong, you're not afraid of him, you know how to defend yourself, and you are ready to do so. In a nutshell, the manipulator will think you are potentially dangerous, and if you think it's desirable, he will eventually be ready to negotiate something with you.

Responding quickly and well does not mean you have to improvise. Learn through your experiences. Make short sentences and stay in limbo, you do not have to justify having a different opinion than his. Stay polite, do not be aggressive, be humorous, but above all avoid being drawn into the manipulator's game by unnecessarily pursuing the discussion.

In order to respond well, one must be able to show enough strength to be heard, but without exaggerating, so as to be respected without being feared.

Responding quickly and well is not a technique usable on demand. It all depends on the manipulator and the circumstances. More than a tool, it is a state of mind that allows one (by responding quickly and with a power slightly below that of the manipulator) to gauge the appropriate response at the moment when it is needed.

Limited Refusal

When we are asked for something, we do not have to accept or refuse it as a whole. There are always things that we can accept and others that we can refuse.

A friend asks me to lend him a sum of money because he has run out and his banker calls him every day. Instead of saying no, I can make the following proposal, "I understand that you need this money and I want to help you, but I can only help for three months because after that I need to pay my taxes. If you do not pay me back in time, I will be in the same situation you are in. That's what I can do for you. Now it's up to you to see."

The Rules of the Limited Refusal

Reformulate the request of the manipulator as you have understood it. "If I understand correctly you would like me to..." In no case should it be a judgment. It should simply be to check that he and you are talking about the same thing. This also has the benefit of eliminating any innuendo and anything unsaid.

Express your partial refusal starting with the positive aspect which will then be legitimized by your restrictions: "I am willing but... I agree on the condition that..." For the manipulator, the partial refusal is closer to an outright acceptance than a refusal.

Place the manipulator at the foot of the wall and ask him to respond to your proposal. "What do you think? That's what I can do, it's up to you! Now it is you who can decide..."

The objective of the limited refusal is not to defeat the manipulator. Where possible, it is a question of making sure that everyone benefits while the other person does not feel wronged. This is called a win-win operation.

The Ten Commandments

All the previous steps are indispensable. Most of the time, they are enough to put an end to small manipulations. But it is also possible that the manipulator will return to the request.

For example, a charming manipulator to whom you have just said no can try to make you feel guilty by retorting, "I thought you were a friend, you have no heart, I can not count on you!" If he sees that it works, he will continue to blame you until he gets what he wants. But if you hold on to and legitimize your refusal by answering his retort, you will end up winning. For example, you might say, "You can see things like that, but I see them differently!" You have affirmed your right to think and reason for yourself instead of resonating with the thoughts of others.

The more one is sure of oneself, the more confident one is in the legitimacy of one's point of view, and the more one can oppose and easily say what one thinks. This assurance will force the manipulator to respect us, to fear us secretly, even to avoid us altogether. It is this indifference to what he can say or do that will eventually discourage him when we are able to adopt that attitude long enough.

To facilitate this legitimacy and to be less vulnerable to the guilt that is a weapon common to all manipulators, here are your main rights that it is good to know and reread regularly.

The Ten Commandments to become indifferent to manipulation:

1. I have the right not to be perfect.

2. I have the right not to be logical.

3. I have the right not to know something.

4. I have the right not to deceive myself.

5. I have the right to have my personal opinion.

6. I have the right not to please everyone.

7. I have the right sometimes to be indifferent to certain problems.

8. I have the right to change my mind or not to have an opinion on something.

9. I have the right not to justify myself.

10. I have the right to think of myself.

Continue this list by adding all the rights that you dare not grant or that you want to claim. Post this list or just these Ten Commandments in a place where you are sure you can read them again every day.

Thus, you will become more and more indifferent to the arguments of the manipulators.

Inventing New Weapons

To find the strength and the means to fight against manipulation, one can imagine how someone else would act in our place. Regardless of the person, the key is to find and use another point of view that will allow us both to escape our reflexes of submission and imagine other solutions.

Find a situation of authoritarian manipulation and ask yourself: In this situation, who would be able to defend themselves against the manipulator? What would he say? What would he do?

The answer may be a person (his superior, his wife, or another such person as would resist him), or a higher authority concept such as a lawyer, a leader, a policeman, a nurse, a gangster, or anyone else who, in your opinion, could dominate the manipulator without any problem. In any case, imagine what this person (real or not) would say or do to master the manipulator. This information is valuable because it awakens unsuspected talents and resources within you.

Chapter 10 - Identifying Manipulator Types

Have you ever felt a sudden lack of self-confidence or, worse, this curious and agonizing impression of not knowing how to communicate? Have you ever been deafened by doubt about your skills or qualities? Have you ever been inhabited by that feeling of inferiority that paralyzes you, chills your blood and prevents you from reacting normally? If you have ever experienced this kind of situation, it is because you have been the victim of type III manipulation and placed in the line of sight of a manipulator.

We remember that the second type of manipulator is a selfish or egocentric person who thinks only of his interests, without worrying about the consequences. But the type III manipulator, which is also called the manipulator, has a very different characteristic intention. His only goal is to destroy. Everything he undertakes is meant to kill you, to ruin what you do, or to destroy an aspect of your personality that does not suit him.

The manipulator is characterized both by his will to harm and by a formidable ability to conceal. This is why many people do not trust him or take him for another.

The manipulator does not display distinctive signs, and his perversity does not necessarily read on his face. He is a true chameleon that hides behind deceptive appearances to better destroy. He can take the appearance of a parent who is "overprotective" and who, out of selfishness, prevents his child from becoming independent. The manipulator could be a nice grandmother who, secretly, gives money to her little girl who is in rehab to, supposedly, "help her hold on". It can also be a mistress, a lover, a boss, a neighbor, a teacher, or a long-time friend. In the cozy atmosphere of the offices, it is the collaborator willing to do anything to take your place or that colleague who seeks to devalue you because your expertise is shady.

His intention is to destroy. Sometimes it may bring him something, but in this case, it's a secondary benefit because what he's essentially aiming for is the destruction of who you are, what you do, or the other of your behaviors.

Illustration

It is through these situations and testimonies that we will examine the harmful activity of a type III manipulator.

• A man wanted his son, Jean, to succeed him by also becoming a doctor at all costs. When Jean announced his desire to leave school to become a musician, his father did everything to break that dream and bring his son back to what he thought was the right path. He tried to persuade his son that he was right in seeking to destroy this vocation. "I did it for your sake, you'll thank me later," he told him then. But what he put his son through was a terrible ordeal that almost drove Jean to suicide, as he felt rejected, devalued, ridiculed, humiliated, and disavowed deep within himself.

• A husband insidiously belittles his wife, Christelle, so that she stays at home. He has nothing against her. He simply does not want her to become independent because it's not how things are done in his family, and he earns enough to make her happy. As she does not agree, he will do everything to prove (by demeaning and humiliating her) that she is unable to do without him. From his point of view, he thinks he is acting justly and in the interest of his wife. But one can easily imagine that Christelle does not see things in the same way.

• A department head, who confronts and belittles a better-performing collaborator than himself, does not necessarily feel particular hatred toward this person. He is simply trying to break the person because he feels they are a danger to him and the only way he can defend his own mediocrity is to belittle them, to diminish them, or to put him in his place so that he does not do not encroach on the department head's work. He destroys what seems to him to be a threat that could prevent him from continuing to dominate the situation. In return, the employee can talk about bullying.

The type III manipulator is a weak man who, when he feels he is in danger, tries to diminish others. He advances masked. Where a normal person tries to surpass himself to become stronger (than whatever threatens him), the manipulator has no other resource than to weaken or treacherously destroy everything that worries him.

He destroys for the sake of destruction. He is mean and does not allow others to exist on their own. He wants to control everything. We cannot impress him. It makes you feel that you are small, weak, shabby; it turns you into a "mop", it tramples you and makes you incapable of any development.

He destroys you by giving you the impression that it is for your good, but we feel very bad in his presence. We cannot win. We are not recognized for what we would like to be. He does not listen to you, and his criticism is never constructive. When he says something, it's always negative. With him, one feels humiliated, discouraged, and degraded. He is a "mental assassin" and life with him is like slavery.

When someone is suspected of being a manipulator, the only way to know what one really has to do is to use the confidence test (see Chapter 3). This test separates the appearance and truth of the situation and highlights the perverse maneuvers that the manipulator uses against us.

Harassment and Concealed Manipulation

Type III manipulation often goes unnoticed by those who experience it. This is called harassment or hidden manipulation. A large number of victims are thus abused and destroyed without their knowledge by the deceit and duplicity of a manipulator. After two pregnancies, Chloe cannot seem to get back to the weight she was as a young girl. She explains her fight against the pounds:

"When I discover a new diet, I hasten to try it. I am sure this time will be the right one. I do what it takes, and I feel good. I have a clear mind, I am dynamic. Sometimes I even go back to playing sports. I do everything I can without effort, and I start losing weight. And then, brutally, without my understanding why, I fall back into the fog. I have no courage, I ruminate on the same black thoughts, I do not do anything, I am exhausted, and I spend my time sleeping. Then, seeing all the tasks accumulating around the apartment, I feel guilty and without realizing it, I start eating again. I call myself names while looking at my belly and my thighs in the mirror of the bathroom. Every day, I decided that, the next day, I will put myself firmly on a diet and that this time I will get there. Today, I am completely desperate because despite all my attempts, every time I get on the scale, I can see that I still gained weight."

While a hidden manipulation is hardly perceptible from the inside, this is not the case when we observe it from the outside. This is what a friend of Chloe tells us about her weight problems:

"I have known Chloe for many years. She was always a little concerned about her weight, but it almost became an obsession from the moment she met Guillaume, her future husband. He is a charming boy, but he attaches great importance to appearances. Since Chloe gained a little weight, having had her children, he frequently comments on it. He always comments nicely, in the tone of the joke, but I think it comes a little too often. I also see that Chloe is touched, even if she pretends to laugh with the others about her 'little bulges' as she says. But I can see that deep down she is hurt when he makes fun of her in public. Moreover, in the days that follow, she regularly buys clothes that are too small, claiming that she is going to lose weight. The other night, I was at home, and he did not stop criticizing a common friend who had grown enormously. He told multiple bad jokes about his plumpness and talked about the contempt he had for people who do not know how to control their weight. When Chloe came out of the room with tears in her eyes, he suddenly changed the subject of conversation. Everyone was embarrassed, but he did not seem to notice. The worst part was that he seemed satisfied with what he had just done as if it were a good joke. I thought about Chloe, and it was really awful to see how happy he looked."

A manipulator can be extremely pleasant and user-friendly. By appearing charming, playing on someone's guild, or using a respectable or simply authoritarian position, he creates a mirage that deceives his victims and prevents them from seeing that behind his disguise of the moment, hides a purpose that is invariably destructive and harmful. Moreover, it is very difficult to blame him for the behavior because he always has an excuse to justify himself: "I am only following the instructions. I do not have the right to disobey. I only did my duty. I acted believing it was the right thing to do. It was a joke."

To be sure, we can examine (below) the two sets of symptoms that signify the presence of a manipulator. The first contains the essentials of what one feels when one is a direct victim of a manipulator and the second enumerates what one perceives as a mere observer of a hidden manipulation.

Internal Symptoms of Concealed Manipulation

These are the main internal signals that can be seen when one is a victim of type III manipulation. These symptoms are far more indicative of the presence of a manipulator than the analysis of his words or deeds:

- I alternate moments of enthusiasm and discouragement. I often feel a sense of guilt or doubt.

- I find it difficult to defend myself or counterattack. I feel a sudden loss of confidence in myself.

- I sometimes feel that I am "drained" of my energy. I feel physical or mental discomfort in the presence of someone.

- That person belittles me one way or another. It is impossible to impress or affect her.

- There is always a form of ambiguity between what she does and what she says. I am not well in my head or in my body when I am around that person.

If you have at least three symptoms, there is a good chance that you have been the victim of such manipulation. When all five symptoms are reached, manipulation is certain, and you should focus on finding out for sure who the manipulator is and how he proceeds.

Use the confidence test (chapter 3) to examine people in your immediate or indirect circle, in relation to what happens to you. Do not hesitate to ask for advice or help!

Generally, someone with an outside perspective can find out much more easily because they will often notice things that one who is a victim and who lives things from within misses.

External Symptoms

The following are the main symptoms that can occur when hidden manipulation is observed from an outside perspective:

- Irrational behavior

- Bad recurring atmosphere

- Discord between people

- People are often sick

- General or chronic discouragement

- Mental and physical exhaustion

Behaviors Are Irrational

This means that people behave strangely. They do things that a sensible person would not do. Due to the active and harmful presence of a manipulator, the victim embarks on utopian projects that are unrealistic or far beyond his/her abilities or skills.

Sometimes, some people succeed in what they do. But for more than 99 percent, it is a failure that awaits them. Many teenagers thus adopt irrational behaviors to show their independence and oppose the guardianship of their parents. This does not mean that parents are true malicious manipulators, but it is a sign that teenagers see them as such.

The Bad Mood

If high fever is symptomatic of the flu, a bad state of mind or a heavy atmosphere also may indicate a type III manipulation. Unconsciously, we feel that something is wrong. Relationships are tense, and we deplore the situation.

In the presence of such manipulation, we are often mistaken as guilty and wrongly accused that the manipulator is us. He is a real expert at confusing simple things and disturbing people's judgment. That's why it's so important to know the anatomy and physiology of type III manipulation before you can begin to resist it effectively.

Illness

In the workplace, when one observes that employees frequently take sick leaves, there are many accidents at work, or there are many requests for transfer or departure, one can be certain that there is a type III manipulator. It's his way of getting rid of those who bother him. In the presence of a heavy and deleterious atmosphere, it is normal that the bodies of the people concerned eventually crack. To contract a disease and to be the victim of an accident are unfortunately the most common reactions of those who undergo too much a concealed manipulation without being able to defend against it.

It is the same in the family environment when, coincidentally, we find that all members of the same family are chronically ill. In such cases, the disease is, again, the direct result of manipulation.

Another remarkable signal is that the manipulator is the only one who is not sick. But this is not infallible because the manipulator sometimes invokes a so-called disease to enslave better or destroy those around him. In the latter case, this kind of "Aunt Danièle" will be unmasked because of a surprising resistance and a great ability to survive (against all the odds).

Discouragement

The manipulator is surrounded by unlucky people who are as enthusiastic as they are discouraged. When manipulation is rife in the world of work, we notice that the best are leaving or looking to leave.

Concealed manipulation is fertile ground for fiascos and repeated failures. When he has the means, the manipulator sabotages the activity of those around him by giving imprecise orders, contradictory instructions, or simply by not giving them the means to succeed.

In private life, his relatives are depressed, sick or un-ambitious. Generally, they miss everything they undertake. The hidden manipulator likes to devalue others or diminish the value of their efforts. Whatever you do, you will never be up to it. If you ever are, he will come to disturb you by pretending to help you, or he will discreetly put sticks in the wheels.

This kind of manipulator will never tell you that you are doing something right. He does not know how to congratulate, and we must not wait for any acknowledgment from him. On the other hand, he knows how to find any little detail that ruins your efforts or proves that he is superior to you and knows better than you. In short, it makes you think that you could succeed in what you want to do.

By discouraging his entourage, the manipulator keeps them helpless or mediocre, which allows him to feel stronger and to establish his power, control, and supremacy more securely.

Exhaustion

The mere presence of a manipulator can be enough to drain you of your energy. It is normal to experience moments of despondency or discouragement, this happens to everyone. When this exhaustion becomes chronic or occurs for no apparent reason, it is a very strong sign that may reveal the existence of hidden manipulation.

If you regularly feel "gutted", find out who is always present in those moments. There is a good chance that you will discover a manipulator that you might never have suspected otherwise.

But before you say anything, submit the person to the confidence test.

Depression can also come from a succession of failures. At more than 38 years old, Claudine has been suffering since childhood from her mother's lack of consideration. Her mother has always considered her a bit simple because she had trouble attending school. To receive a little of this love that is so lacking and also to show that she is someone worthwhile, Claudine is doing everything she can to please her mother. She goes to see her every day. She does her housework and accompanies her to shop at least once a week. Her mother finds this normal and does not feel the need to thank her with a word, a gesture, or a gift. On the other hand, she phones her for hours to complain about her health or her problems with her neighbors. Patiently, Claudine listens to her and tries to comfort her. Obviously, the mother does everything to come and live with her daughter, but Claudine turns a deaf ear. She is torn between her need for recognition that would push her to take her mother home, and her need to live an independent life with her husband and children.

Blind to this manipulation and unable to say no to her manipulative mother, Claudine is exhausted in responding to the ever-growing demands of a mother who is becoming more and more of a burden and who complains to anyone who wants to hear that her daughter "abandoned" her. However, she continues to serve as a servant because she is still unconsciously waiting for a sign of recognition from her mother. Unfortunately for Claudine, this liberating signal will never come.

Feeling more and more helpless, useless, and worthless, Claudine finally sinks into a deep depression. This will allow her mother to shamelessly assert that her daughter is definitely worthless and cannot be counted on under any circumstances.

This example shows us that when exhaustion, discouragement, and sickness affect the same person, it is clear evidence that hidden manipulation is occurring.

The manipulator always thinks he is right. He never questions himself or changes his mind. It is the others who are wrong, never him. It's impossible! Whoever ignores this incapacity can only be exhausted in wanting to change someone who absolutely does not want to.

Moreover, if you make him read this book, he would find it interesting or very useful... for others! But he will never feel concerned and will not recognize himself.

Conclusion

The manipulator is like a dark cloud that prevents the sun's rays from reaching us. As long as it dominates us or we stay "below", we feel bad, we do stupid things, we're confused, and we go around in circles. But by cutting off all relationships of dependence or by completely breaking with the one that ruins our lives, we come out of its nefarious darkness to find the warm rays of peace, freedom, and intelligence.

The Essentials of This Book:

• When one realizes that the manipulator is a weak person and a coward who abuses the power that one lends him to belittle and enslave, us and when one discovers that the thirst for being oneself is stronger than his threats, his weapons, or his blackmail, then the anxiety disappears.

• By going beyond one's own fear, one goes beyond one's intimidation, and one discovers that in reality, one does not risk much in opposing a manipulator. Awakening from the nightmare that he makes us live in, we understand that he is afraid of others and draws his power from our ignorance of his true weakness. One can then begin to react, to defend oneself, and regain the power to say no to him.

• Contrary to appearances, the manipulator knows himself incapable of overcoming others if he is uncovered. That's why his weapons are lies, cunning, and slander. We cannot impress him. He will never acknowledge his wrongdoing, and he will refuse to be helped or changed.

• He paralyzes us. Even when we suffer his blows, we do not dare to fight back for fear of hypothetical reprisals or for fear of hurting him, especially when we know him well. The biggest mistake is to believe that time will fix everything, or that the manipulator will eventually change, understand, or get bored. But that hardly ever happens.

• The weaknesses of the Type III manipulator are within his strengths. As long as we believe in the blackmail of his threats, we complain, but we do not dare to react. The reality is that it dominates us only as long as we fear it.

• When one discovers that he draws his power from ignorance of his true weakness, paralyzing fear disappears. We know that he is helpless against direct opposition and counter-attacks and that he can only run away from those who dare to challenge him. In these conditions, one is ready to say no to him.

• It is time to organize our defense and to counter-attack. In addition to the tools used against Type II manipulation, there are special techniques to stand up and defeat the Type III manipulator.

• Observing and understanding what is happening brings a release. To perceive the manipulator as they give you the courage to dare to attack.

- Dare to challenge him! Show him that you do not fear him. Do not be afraid to ridicule him but never humiliate him. Avoid devaluing him or using guilt because then he will advantageously position himself as a victim. If you are persuasive enough and insistent, his cowardice will do the rest, and he will leave you alone.

- If you have to attack him, do it, but make sure you have enough ammo! Find out exactly what he's doing and expose his misdeeds in the presence of the witnesses concerned. Accumulate concrete evidence against him, then clearly point out what's wrong. Prevent him from spreading rumors and, if you can, institute very strict rules to control him and neutralize his harmful actions. Do not stop before he bends or breaks. In some cases, it is also necessary to know how to ask for help because the fight is often very hard, and nothing is ever gained in advance.

- Break off the relationship! Sometimes you have to know how to cut communication with the manipulator completely. The price of independence can be heavy to pay. But it is up to everyone to determine what they are willing to sacrifice to live in peace, free and serene.

- It would be an oversimplification to think of the manipulator as a big bad wolf and see us as innocent victims with pure and unblemished hearts. If we are more or less regularly victims of manipulators, this is rarely due to chance. When we always encounter the same obstacles or the same difficulties, we must know how to seek the help of competent people to help us erase or modify the sensitive areas of our past that make us vulnerable to manipulation.

We now know that the manipulator does not question himself and that he is incapable of change. Do not be like him! Let us adapt by finding and using the appropriate means to no longer remain powerless, to strengthen ourselves, and to no longer let ourselves be destroyed by manipulators.

It was the goal of this book to bring information, exercises, and tools to those who feel helpless or manipulative and who never want to be left behind.